# The Apostolic Faith
## Protestants and Roman Catholics

Frederick W. Norris

A Michael Glazier Book
THE LITURGICAL PRESS
Collegeville, Minnesota

A Michael Glazier Book published by The Liturgical Press

Cover design by Greg Becker

1     2     3     4     5     6     7     8     9

**Library of Congress Cataloging-in-Publication Data**

Norris, Frederick, 1941–
     The apostolic faith : Protestants and Roman Catholics
/ Frederick W. Norris.
          p.     cm.
     "A Michael Glazier book."
     Includes bibliographical references and index.
     ISBN 0-8146-5029-5
     1. Fundamentalism.   2. Evangelicalism—United States.   3. Norris,
Frederick, 1941– .   4. Fundamentalist churches—Relations—
Catholic Church.   5. Evangelicalism—Relations—Catholic Church.
6. Catholic Church—Relations—Fundamentalist churches.   7. Catholic
Church—Relations—Evangelicalism.   8. United States—Church
history—20th century.   I. Title.
BT82.2.N687   1992
270—dc20                                                    92-19536
                                                                   CIP

*To*
*the living memory of*
*a remarkable catholic Christian*
*Dean Everest Walker*

*and*

*the living presence of*
*the Cistercian community at*
*the Abbey of Our Lady of New Clairvaux*
*Vina, California*

# Contents

# Preface

When my son brought me his portable phone with a call from Joseph Kelly, I was in the back yard splitting wood. Joe, a friend for nearly a decade, asked if I considered myself an evangelical Protestant. I hesitated and then replied that a number of my friends and foes would see me as such, although I personally preferred the name Christian since I could make sense of it. I finally agreed that most people would consider me a conservative Protestant, probably an Evangelical, although I thought of myself as a free-church catholic.

That apparently was good enough for the department and the university, for after reviewing my academic credentials they named me the Walter and Mary Tuohy Distinguished Visiting Professor of Religious Studies for the Fall of 1988 at John Carroll University. My assignment was to introduce a primarily Roman Catholic audience from the university and the city to these strange Protestants found both in Cleveland and on so many television programs. I taught a course for undergraduates on televangelism and gave six lectures with the title "The Apostolic Faith: Protestant Evangelicals and Roman Catholics."

For the publication of those lectures I have changed the title to "Protestants" so that some comments on Fundamentalists could be more properly included. To describe Fundamentalists I need to refer to mainline Protestantism and thus can use the word without a qualifier even though the emphasis is on conservatism. I also added an introduction to my method of dealing with such issues, a chapter on the Nicene-Constantinopolitan

Creed and one on worship and life. Furthermore I have divided the material into two sections: Protestantism and catholic Christian Faith. It is the latter which all Christians seek to believe.

My thanks are here expressed to Professor Kelly, the Religious Studies Department of John Carroll University, and the Tuohy family for making the semester not only possible but delightful. I also enjoyed the hospitality to strangers offered by the David Mason family, my hosts during the semester.

I am also most appreciative of Ben Cachiaras, Stanley Hauerwas, Susan Higgins, Thomas C. Oden, and Fred P. Thompson who read early drafts of all or part of this volume and Robert Parsley, my research assistant, who read it and prepared the index. Their acceptance gave me strength to continue. Finally I want to thank Paul Marvin, a seminary student at Emmanuel School of Religion who began his life in a faithful, nurturing Roman Catholic home and continued toward the priesthood. After several wrenching months he left that goal, married, and now pursues his education toward ministry outside Roman Catholicism. He continues to concentrate upon catholic Christian Faith from within what many would name a conservative Protestant context yet with a compassionate eye for his parents' heritage. His sensitivity to the issues raised in this book has measurably improved it.

# Introduction

"But Professor Norris, that is anecdotal!"

The pained face of the professor who made that comment changed many of my views on the nature of theology. I was visiting a university during a leave from my regular teaching duties and sitting in a class on fundamental theology taught by a Roman Catholic. The course dealt with the field similar to what Protestants often call apologetics, that is, how do I explain the grounds for my faith to those inside and outside the Christian faith. The professor had asked each of us why we were taking the class. When it came my turn, I told a story. Recently I had been traveling in England and had met a young American student on the train. I asked her what her plans were for the year and she indicated that she was to be a fellowship student in chemistry at one of the British universities. We talked for some time about her background, her sight-seeing trips, and her goals for this year abroad. Eventually she asked me who I was and what I did. I told her I was a theologian. She drew back, blinked, and asked, "Why would someone like you be interested in religion of all things?"

Retelling the story was my way of saying that I hoped on the basis of this seminar in fundamental theology to be better equipped to respond to her initial reaction and to the series of questions which followed. The professor, however, expected his students to have some particular philosophical or academic theological problem that drew them to the course. I certainly had a number of those problems, but uppermost in my mind was the young woman. I thought mentioning her was appropriate. He did not.

I mulled over his reaction for the entire semester and finally decided that anyone who could not see the relevance of the contact with that student, indeed the importance of anecdote for the discussion of Christian faith, must not have understood God's action in the history of Israel, the incarnation of the Son in a common human life, and the leadership of the Spirit in the everyday existence of the Church. There was much to learn from this learned man, but he obviously had great trouble with biblical and historical studies since they so often are concerned with story and history, indeed with tales, parables, and anecdotes. It was almost a knee-jerk reaction for this philosopher of religion to reject an anecdotal reply, to refuse the particular in the name of the universal, but the implications of such rejection were significant and severe.

When a number of years later I was asked to be the Tuohy Professor at John Carroll University, it was a simple task to employ a number of anecdotes in order to communicate my concern for relations between Roman Catholics and conservative Protestants, both Evangelicals and Fundamentalists. The easiest way to let a largely Roman Catholic audience know the difference between a Fundamentalist and an Evangelical, and at the same time to introduce my particular ethos as the lecturer, was to tell stories about my grandfather and my father. Obviously public evening lectures become more effective if they are somewhat lively and offer tales which penetrate memory. Trying to listen to a speaker after an eight-hour day is hard work. I concentrated on the Bible and the Nicene-Constantinopolitan Creed as points of reference for things held in common by these sub-groups of the Christian community and I attempted to intersperse the lectures with stories and humor to keep us all awake.

When the time came to turn those lectures into a book, the immediate temptation was to switch to another style, the more academic one that I have used in other publications. For both good and ill, I have resisted. Some scholars may well find the level of argument in these chapters to be below the standards they have accepted as customary. This book is unabashedly popular—at least I hope it is—without assuming that a general audience could not grapple with certain theological points. Although there is more than a bit of usual historical and systematic argument, the lecture style called for some light comic relief. The attempt was and is to speak clearly, carefully, and often in anecdotal fashion to the type of audience which attended the lectures.

Anecdotes at times are considered the "puns" of history, the table scraps. But there is a sense in which a well-placed anecdote can accomplish in short span and memorable manner what description and sequential argument cannot. Interestingly, anecdotes are often used to depict character, *ethos*. And it is precisely character that some important defenders of narrative theology have suggested as one vital aspect of the Christian good news.[1] Why are tales, stories, and anecdotes such important forms in Scripture and the history of the Church? Perhaps because the personal nature of deity, the humanity of the incarnate Christ, and the people of God resist depiction in other ways. Indeed far afield from theological concerns, Isaac D'Israeli in a small dissertation on anecdotes pointed out their strengths: their relationship to history, to character, and to the common and the bizarre in life.[2]

There is, however, more involved in the choice of this popular, anecdotal style than might be expected from a Tennessean whom some describe as a conservative Protestant. First, Christian spirituality has often begun, been enriched and been maintained through the anecdotes about saints. The sayings of the desert fathers in a number of language traditions—Greek, Latin, Coptic, Syriac, etc.—involve small vignettes which can be cryptic. They are not narratives; indeed they depend on the knowledge of larger Christian narrative for understanding. But that whole monastic tradition does not teach one how to know God by providing only systematic, theological instruction; in fact much early Christian theology which develops hard arguments grows

1. Hans Frei, *The Identity of Jesus Christ: The Hermeneutical Bases of Dogmatic Theology* (Philadelphia: Fortress Press, 1975) and *The Eclipse of Biblical Narrative: A Study in Eighteenth and Nineteenth Century Hermeneutics* (New Haven: Yale University Press, 1974). For a good introduction to the wide concerns of narrative theology see Stanley Hauerwas and L. Gregory Jones, *Why Narrative? Readings in Narrative Theology* (Grand Rapids, Mich.: William B. Eerdmans, 1989).

2. Isaac D'Israeli, *A Dissertation on Anecdotes* (London: C. & G. Kearsley and J. Murray, 1793; rpt. New York: Garland Publishing, 1972).

out of monastic spirituality.[3] Roman Catholic and Eastern Orthodox monastic communities have read the lives of the saints during quiet meals so that the actual living of the gospel rather than the apparent thinking about the gospel became clear. Dietrich Bonhoeffer's *Life Together* gives some indication that such interests need not be completely lost in the Protestant heritage.[4] Yet for the concerns of this present exercise, the deep roots of such anecdotally taught spirituality in Roman Catholicism are in themselves part of one tradition which Protestant Evangelicals can share. Evangelicals from the holiness traditions have a spirituality that feeds on anecdotes and sees faith formation as dependent upon such stories. Furthermore important insights can be gained by considering whether the influence of a Fundamentalist like Francis Schaeffer depends completely upon his ability to argue for a clear, propositional conception of truth—where he can be so unclear—or upon the deep spirituality which marked his relationships with others, particularly at L'Abri. The latter tradition was filled with anecdotes and is itself passed on anecdotally.

A second stream, not dependent upon Christian spirituality, also strengthens a concern for narrative and anecdote as broader ways of reasoning. Stephen Toulmin, in his *Cosmopolis,* cogently argues that the usual conception of modernity in which he lived in the 1930s and 1940s has crumbled. The search for the uncontested foundation of knowledge, which so occupied the seventeenth-century philosopher, Descartes, and gave modern thought its form, lies in disarray. The separation of the rational and the emotional, the disdain for the particular and historical as opposed to the universal, the division of subject and object, the distinction between human action and natural causation, indeed a number of conundrums which marked academic thought up into the 1960s have collapsed.[5] Thus the particularistic biographical sketches of this introduction and the uses of anecdote and humor throughout are not necessarily gauche mistakes. If Toulmin

---

3. See Roberta Bondi, *To Love as God Loves: Conversations with the Early Church* (Philadelphia: Fortress Press, 1987).

4. Dietrich Bonhoeffer, *Life Together,* trans. with intro. by John Doberstein (New York: Harper, 1954).

5. Stephen Toulmin, *Cosmopolis: The Hidden Agenda of Modernity* (New York: The Free Press, 1990).

and others who attack foundationalism are correct,[6] broader, rhetorical forms of argument so prevalent in antiquity and the Renaissance must be reintroduced not merely within theology, but also within science, mathematics, art, literature, into every discipline of human understanding. In that case this present exercise is also an attempt to fit into such an old but new mold. It rejoices as does Toulmin in the model of Erasmus, who as a Christian humanist drank deeply from the font of classical knowledge, both Christian and Graeco-Roman. Erasmus was influential on three fronts: Roman Catholic, Magisterial Reformation, and Anabaptist. His waning influence and death left those three traditions to begin modernity by castigating each other's insights. Roman Catholics and Magisterial Reformers, who had access to political power, tried to annihilate Anabaptists and had considerable success. Then they turned on each other only to produce the Thirty Years War. According to Toulmin, it was precisely that devastating tragedy which formed much of the context for Descartes' attempt to avoid history and get to the universal foundation of knowledge. Descartes fled to Holland both to avoid the less widespread religious strife in France and the ravages of the war in Germany.

It is thus appropriate for someone like myself from an Anabaptist heritage, which depended so much on Erasmus' editions of the New Testament, his grammatical method and thus a type of Roman Catholicism, to offer some comments about contemporary affairs. Perhaps in a small way this volume can help Roman Catholics and conservative Protestants look at each other without the blinders of sixteenth and seventeenth-century theological and political acrimony. Perhaps it can weaken the philosophical, literary, artistic, and social tunnel vision which the Enlightenment created. If modernity, as Toulmin describes it, is dead or dying, then Fundamentalist attempts to restore the foundations of universal knowledge and evangelize the world through a "modern" apologetic are doomed to failure. The same can be said for staid Roman Catholic fundamental theology which does not recognize

6. See Ronald Thiemann, "Radiance and Obscurity in Biblical Narrative," *Scriptural Authority and Narrative Interpretation,* ed. Garrett Green (Philadelphia: Fortress Press, 1987) 26, for both a short, clear paragraph describing foundationalism and a list of the literature, n. 12, which attacks that position.

the burial of foundationalism. Roman Catholics and Evangelical Protestants must look at each other's sub-traditions of Christianity with an historical and contextual eye. All can recognize and confess that neither Protestant nor Catholic tradition so captures the truth and justice of Christian faith and doctrine that another Thirty Years War is in order. Belfast is not our model. The recognition and confession of such weaknesses are not based on a softening of religious commitment or an abandoning of theological positions. It is firmly grounded in perceptions of life which tell us clearly that all our doctrinal positions are "broken lights" and that our concern for each other is a search for "mended lives."[7] Each of our perspectives and views is historically conditioned. We can argue about their merit, but we cannot assume that there will be "self-evident truths" or "universally accepted foundations" out there somewhere for us to claim.

Some of the great fathers of the Church understood much of this and thus were part of the heritage which the Renaissance recovered. Logic and rhetoric worked together for them. Although Plato was often highly regarded, theologians like the Cappadocians could well see the value of the Aristotelian heritage with its empirical science and its view of philosophical rhetoric. For nearly all these ancient lights—broken though they may be—God in his nature, even in his grace, was far beyond our ability to understand in any complete way. The problem was not merely how to express God as Plato had suggested in the *Timaeus,* but even how one might go about forming conceptions of him. According to Gregory Nazianzen, called "the Theologian" by ancient and Eastern tradition, any theology relies on models, analogies, images and thus in many ways must resemble or be poetry. Only those who do not understand the limitation of human intellect could suggest that they fully know the nature of God.[8]

In important ways, then, the insights of significant fathers of the Church and important students of contemporary learning and

7. See the brilliant account by Rowan A. Greer, III, *Broken Lights and Mended Lives* (University Park, Penn.: Pennsylvania State University Press, 1986) that highlights these central features of patristic thought and practice.

8. See *Faith Gives Fullness to Reasoning: The Five Theological Orations of Gregory Nazianzen,* intro. and comm. by Frederick W. Norris, trans. Lionel Wickham and Frederick Williams (Leiden: E. J. Brill, 1991).

culture are agreed. Whether as Roman Catholics or Evangelical Protestants, we belong to the more basic community of those who seek to be catholic Christians. We pray, we preach, we witness and we discuss. We seek the best "broken lights" which our minds and experience can uncover. We can argue about which are better and perhaps even leave behind our first impressions of things that appear so bizarre in order to find some merit in their presence. We must take advantage of the heritage of less-heated table talk which marked much of the Renaissance and is or can be a feature of our contemporary era at the same time that we do not create meatless soups called "natural religion" where anything anyone dumps in the pot will be consumed. We must talk with each other even in hard ways about how we need each other in the search for catholic Christianity. At the same time we must confess our inability to find a universal, foundational statement of Christian faith or anything else. Recognizing that we now "see in a glass darkly" and only later "face to face," only then "knowing as we are known," we can confess that if our views are that partial, talking with other Christians is enriching as well as it is challenging. Indeed conversations among Catholics and Protestants are quite a small circle when we consider how many humans seek a way to God.

Thus this present exercise is neither a packed, systematic argument in defense of the universal truth of Christianity couched in the terms of modernity, nor a full account of the importance of humor to story, story to character, character to history, and history to revelation and theology. It is a much more partial and sober attempt to ease Christians from formerly warring camps into constructive light, even if that light shines dimly through a crack. It is the telling of stories, a telling built on the assumption that the sense of things can be communicated and the mood improved if we talk turkey and swap some yarns.

\* \* \*

Life can be bizarre. Thus it is often happily surprising and frightfully disillusioning. We try to impose an order and sense the disorder. Our various personalities and experiences lead us to react differently to its demands. Some are happy with the familiar; others live for adventure. Some are tolerant of change or challenge; others fight against the unusual and the unknown. For these and other reasons, any definition of "Fundamentalist" or "Evangelical" is difficult to attain. Movements which entail so many theological, sociological, political, and intellectual details are not easy to describe. These terms also have relatively substantial histories that spread across many continents. Thus my initial task is to introduce some limitations. I intend to focus primarily on the development of Fundamentalism and Evangelicalism in the United States during the twentieth century. The first two chapters describe these phenomena in ways that, I hope, will make them recognizable. If you have grown up in such groups, I may pluck chords which make music or create painful vibrations. If you have not come from within such circles, your reaction will often be: "How bizarre." You well may be right. Flannery O'Conner, the Southern Roman Catholic writer, told stories of her Protestant Fundamentalist surroundings, not only making them fictional, but also using distortion as a technique. But her characters often have the smell of real life for those who have lived in such situations. Yet the problem with all studies of people and ideas strange to us is that they end up being bizarre. What I shall attempt here is to make these groups intelligible, to create an empathetic, if not a sympathetic, understanding. That is important for at least two reasons. First, devising methods to grasp the significant features of the odd is a lifelong task we all share. Other creatures become curiouser and curiouser, perhaps—God forbid—even we ourselves. Yet compassion for strangers is necessary for human community. Understanding what to accept and what to reject is what gives families, tribes, nations and churches their character. Yet every family, tribe, nation or church has some unusual characteristics and some decidedly odd characters.

Second, the strategy in the last six chapters apparently will involve a great shift, but it is only a superficial change. If together we can recognize and understand the bizarre within others and ourselves, and put those features in their place, perhaps we then can grasp the common characteristics which we share. In 1988 in Cleveland we could argue about the differences between the home town Cleveland Browns and the hated Denver Broncos only to forget that we were talking about football. On occasion it is helpful for Christians who appear so odd to each other to remember that they are Christians. Thus in the last six chapters we will look together at those great features of faith which we all share: the Nicene-Constantinopolitan Creed, God, Christ, the Holy Spirit, the Church, and Worship and Life.

My task in the rest of this introduction is also complicated because I was basically unknown to most who heard the lectures and now probably to you, the reader. After giving me some of your time, you may wish to keep it that way. Because you have not had the opportunity of getting to know me, I have uppermost in my mind the rhetorician's concern for the *ethos* or character of the speaker. How should I introduce myself? My decision then was to talk to my audience in the first lecture and here to talk to you in this introduction about Fundamentalism and Evangelicalism by telling you something about my grandfather and my father. I am interested in giving flesh and bone to the analysis of Fundamentalism and Evangelicalism.

My maternal grandfather, F. S. Dowdy, was a preacher born in northeastern Kentucky. He came from a poor family which had too little time for children. In fact my great-grandfather always left home when it became obvious that great-grandmother was pregnant again. He had no doubt that he was the guilty party, but a pregnancy always angered him. He enjoyed being cared for and had little interest in giving care. My grandfather's first long absence from primary school was to look after his mother while his father had disappeared once again. Grandpa did not have the deep, loving family which he wanted, not even the doting attention of a proud mother. She was too busy with the other children for that.

Grandpa ate the first orange he ever saw just as you would eat an apple. Not strangely he thought it a quite overrated fruit. What fun he had as a child was much like the orange—some sweetness at the core but much bitterness on the way to it. He had to quit school for good at a very young age in spite of his great native intelligence and deep desire to learn. He never lost his love of learning. As time allowed he studied on his own and occasionally as a part-time student in regular colleges or seminaries. He had taken the Kentucky state teachers' examination and had passed. Thus he had become a teacher in a system which had failed to graduate him.

He grew up a tepid Methodist, but became a member of the Church known as the Disciples of Christ through deep study and the following of various debates in communities where he lived. He loved to argue any point, sometimes for the fun of it, but most often for what he saw as the truth of the question at issue. He became a remarkable preacher, both through the development of his oratorical skills by speaking, and through acquisition of homiletical knowledge by studying. After ordination he continued his education on the same piecemeal plan, taking courses as he could. He taught himself Greek, but took Hebrew at Pittsburgh Theological Seminary while he was preaching in that city. He bought books and devoured them. When he died, I received his library, nearly 8,000 volumes primarily devoted to the Bible and theology.

Grandpa was a Fundamentalist. Much of his library contained books on the Modernist-Fundamentalist controversy of the early part of this century. He could not stand the "higher critical" study of Scripture; it was an attack on the truth of the Word of God. Volumes on the inerrancy of Scripture, the historical accuracy of its accounts, the presuppositional tyranny of classical liberal theology and the new modernism, the fallacy of evolution and the truthfulness of the Genesis account, the defense of Jesus' miracles, the historicity of the virgin birth and the resurrection filled many shelves. My first introduction to the great American Fundamentalist teachers: B. B. Warfield and J. Gresham Machen—both professors at Princeton Theological Seminary—came through my grandfather's library. That library also included noted systematic theologians of the generation just preceding the birth of American Fundamentalism, particularly Charles Hodge, again a Princeton professor.

Grandpa's intellectual fairness also meant that I was introduced to the important revilers of Fundamentalism in his library. He had books by the so-called liberals or modernists. Harry Emerson Fosdick was well-represented. Even the non-Christian opponents were present. My acquaintance with H. L. Mencken came through browsing among grandfather's books. Sinclair Lewis' critique of small towns and sex-craving revivalists also could be found in those bookcases.

But it was Scripture which was the mainstay. Biblical commentaries formed a large portion of his personal collection. Teaching and preaching its contents were what made up grandpa's life of public speaking. He tried his best to take Scripture with the utmost seriousness, and like many of us, failed more than once. His love of the Bible bordered on a strange bibliolatry. My mother tells of numerous times in which she was punished for laying something on top of a Bible, not only the one which had a prominent place on the coffee table in the living room, but also any Bible found in the house. Nothing was to be above the Bible. I suspect that only those who come from Roman Catholic or Eastern Orthodox homes with icons of the Blessed Virgin or one of the saints can understand this sense of the physical, sacred presence of a Bible.

For him, Roman Catholicism was a scourge. Its leaders were more honest than many Protestant theologians since they frankly said that they changed the Bible with traditions, while liberal Protestants did the same but denied it. Romanism was not catholic, because it did not represent the universal truth of Christian Faith. It covered over the clarity of Scripture and the simplicity of the gospel with the traditions of men. Ceremonies and mysteries kept the good news from the people. Priests stood in the way of each individual's free access to God through Christ. Popish authoritarianism crushed personal, loving response and replaced it with clannish obedience based on fear. Furthermore, it was totally un-American. No democratic institutions could survive under Rome's leadership as the struggles of such forms of government in Latin America proved. Al Smith's candidacy for the presidency in 1928 had to be opposed, for no thinking person, certainly no Christian, would support a religious control of the state on the basis of both political and theological principles opposed to the heart and soul of our country.

Most of my grandfather's located ministries, that is, the periods when he was the pastor of a local congregation rather than a traveling evangelist, were held in the North, not in the South. Some of them were in smaller communities in Ohio and Pennsylvania, but two substantial ministries were in Cleveland and Pittsburgh. Both those churches were located in urban rather than suburban settings, and were comprised of quite wealthy as well as middle-class people; both grew under his leadership. Although a Kentuckian, he could communicate successfully with Northern urban dwellers, even some of those cities' movers and shakers, not just immigrants from West Virginia. But his pastorates were often short because of his inability to get along well with others over an extended period of time.

Grandpa was a debater, a rationalist fired by deep emotions, who could be quite persuasive. He was the first secretary of a committee forming a conservative convention which marked the beginning of a separation between the Christian Churches and the Disciples of Christ in 1929. His fame as a preacher for revival meetings was widespread among the church group that he served. Even in his seventies, he preached such a revival at the small church I pastored in Oklahoma during the 1960s. He held a group of conservative, Protestant Christians spellbound with his clear presentation, his command of Scripture, and his moving illustrations—all done with few if any notes.

As a young man, when his first chance had come to leave his father and mother, he did just that. He married and formed his own family. The relationship was a good one most of the time although the temperaments of the two were almost diametrically opposed. Grandpa was a star; grandma was a stagehand. She never developed a sense of her own need to be center stage until after their divorce. He never learned to play a small part gracefully. Attraction to other women had been a problem for him. In mid-life when he went on the road as a traveling evangelist, he first divorced my grandmother to marry his song evangelist; then when the scandal cut short his invitations for revival meetings, he tired of the song evangelist. He eventually had four wives, a kind of serial polygamy which he often found some convoluted, "scriptural" way to justify. His brilliant mind, with its interpretive skills and debater's logic, could twist most any theme to his advantage. Graciously his last wife cared for him when he became quite ill, probably with Alzheimer's disease, even to the point that he thought people on television were visitors in his home.

His scandalous divorce had forced him to pastor small churches that had not heard the news. (Our American congregations are self-governing with no authoritative presbytery, bishop, or association to pass on national or regional news.) Eventually he repented his misdeeds, but something remained warped about him which as a young adult even I could see. The Fundamentalist-Modernist battle had scarred him as deeply as had his early childhood experiences. He tried to preach the gospel, to proclaim the grace of God found in Jesus Christ. Often he was successful, for he knew personally how that good news could change a life. He had found release from many difficulties in the love of God. But much of what he spoke was legalistic, not gracious. With his magnificent intelligence he found inferences and evidences, proofs and disproofs, which were often stunning. Yet as a positivist, as someone who lived more by sight and less by faith, he was often troubled. He had fits of depression, one time even leading to hysterical blindness for a few days. He was convinced that there must be clear demonstrations of the truth of the gospel, ones he could find which would turn every rational human to Jesus Christ as Lord and Savior. When doubt confronted him, he was filled with terror. The only way to keep it at bay was to attack its foundations with pounding, systematic logic.

He knew a great deal about doctrine, but too little about believing. He taught well and trusted little, and thus left a heritage of brilliant intellect but personal failure. He fought the fight, but seldom if ever knew the peace of God. I have childhood memories of his warmth and laughter. I still possess a few gifts given out of the deep affection he felt for his children and grandchildren. He gave me a lovely glass horse, which I now display in my home, and taught me the name of Alexander the Great's horse so that as a very small child I could properly pronounce "Bucephalus" and say that was the name of my horse. I astounded the unlearned who responded: "Poor little fellow. He can't talk plain yet." I loved my grandfather and love him still. But sadly much of his legacy I cannot claim.

My father, William O. Norris, had served just after seminary as an assistant minister with my grandfather in order to gain the necessary practical skills from a fine practitioner. Attired in tie and tails, pinstripped pants, and the tall top hat demanded by this rather wealthy and influential congregation in Cleveland during the late 1930s, he learned some of the great weaknesses which marked grandpa's character, but he was not thrown off course by the clear dangers that later became fact. My father had grown up on an Indiana farm just south of Indianapolis in the midst of a family which had long been members of a Disciples of Christ congregation. His people had owned one of the Rush County banks that went under in the depression. Rather than let the community suffer the loss as the law allowed, the family sold their large landholdings at depression prices so that the local folks could get as much on their dollars as possible. No more trips to Paris or degrees from the University of Chicago for the family's maiden aunts. His mother had hidden the shotgun when their farm was sold, because she feared his father's reaction. They made it through those rough times, however, and eventually had a good farm of their own.

In this family grandma was the firebrand and grandpa the cooling water. I stayed summers with them when I was a young lad. I slept on a daybed in the dining room just outside their bedroom, because the downstairs was cooler during those hot months. One of my earliest remembrances of repeated prayers, is "Oh, Lord, please let me go to sleep before they start snoring." God was alive and active for me in a very important way.

Dad had intended to be a farmer and would have been a good one. He still rises before six and fills days with long hours. That farming community and his own family gave him a trust in life and a sense of balance that has stayed with him ever since. Coming to faith was no battle; it was the essential outworking of what he saw around him, both in nature and in people. The examples were not always sterling; he often met sickness and death as farm people do. In his own ministry he has always been impressed with the good in life as he has encountered and has tried to change the evil. During my teenage years I remember his bringing two teenaged girls to our house dressed only in blankets, young women who had been raped by their drunken father and thrown out into the cold northern Ohio winter. I can still feel the pain he felt when a man who was a member of our church stuck a shotgun in his mouth and blew his brains all over the kitchen ceiling just after my father had met with him in his home. I have seen my dad quake in remembering his own walk through the concentration camp at Dachau, where the bodies of the dead had been thrown into piles but not buried, where the decaying flesh and excrement in the barracks came up over his shoe soles. He has led no Pollyannaish existence, but he still finds goodness. More than once I have heard him ask when someone bemoaned the hellishness of life, "Yes, indeed, . . . but where does the good come from?"

My mother, Judy's, faith has been more difficult to achieve. Her father had made her feel unchangeably second-class, just because she was female. He thought that was the biblical teaching. He also worried about the evil influences which could warp her life. Once he burned the dress and shoes grandma had scrimped to buy for a school dance, because such a function was evil. Mother struggled to have a personality, with a father whose Bible—and his father—had put women in their "rightful, lower" place. She battled with brothers who became a college president and a surgeon, the one less than the other. She fought and scrapped and became not only a mother and housewife, but an accomplished accompanist and teacher. Most importantly, however, she grappled with her own fears, her own senses of inadequacy, and built a reservoir of trust. Even now those early experiences can come back with haunting effectiveness, but she usually keeps them at bay.

Both my parents have made education a high priority. Although my mother never finished college, she has read widely and is herself a published writer. (Her mother never fully recovered from the divorce but she did graduate from college in her sixties, an odd occurrence for that time.) My father struggled a bit in his early university career while adjusting from a small county high school. But he became an honors student and a scholarship winner during his seminary career. Yet neither of them has developed the narrow intellectualism which marked my maternal grandfather.

In every pastorate that my parents have served, there have been people who have developed a deeper faith in God and in life. They have sensed that their work place, their home, and their recreation are all aspects of their priesthood. There have been failures; some churches have not been a good match. But most of their ministries were of longer duration, because my parents could lead and persevere. Now in their semi-retirement, people who found God under their leadership come for visits, call, and write.

My father never participated in the Modernist-Fundamentalist debate. He was and is a conservative, biblically-based minister, who preaches and lives a simple Christianity which never marked him or anyone else as a simpleton. He has not found it necessary to fight against every wind of doctrine. He eventually left the Disciples of Christ to work with the Christian Churches as he found the latter more true to his conservative experience. But for years he continued to go to functions of the former group just to keep in touch and by his presence work for Christian unity. Dad assumes that living for Jesus is better than fighting for the faith. For him love is not a conception but a way of existing. Christian doctrine is more what you are and what you do than what you think. He can get angry and take on someone, arguing for an idea which he finds atrocious. But basically he trusts and finds the good.

My grandfather was a Fundamentalist; in some ways my father could be called an Evangelical. He still believes that the Bible is inspired, that its stories are accurate, but in doing research for books he and mother have written together with the titles *What the Bible Says About X,* he knows that not every jot and tittle is in place. The names used and events described in one passage do not exactly fit what is said in another verse. If you talk to him about the Bible, he won't talk to you about errors. It isn't important unless you make it so. The great truths of Scripture are still in place, basically unassailed. God created the heavens and the earth. He led his people into Canaan. Their stories tell us who we are. The prophets spoke to them and speak to us. Jesus was born of a virgin, he taught the truth and did miracles, he died for our sins, he rose from the dead, and will return. The Spirit is alive and living among us. The Church is Christ's body on earth; the gates of hell shall not prevail against it. Dad won't fight you about those things, but he will cajole you. He will preach the word in season and out of season through story, precept, and example.

My father doesn't despise Roman Catholicism, never did and thus is neither clearly Fundamentalist nor Evangelical. If as a Catholic you were to talk with him about things theological, you would find him questioning the function of tradition, the style of worship, the authority of the pope, the place of Mary in the plan of salvation. I can remember funny asides in the 1950s when the American religious movies of the previous decade concentrated on Irish priests: "Are there no Protestant ministers in the land?" But I can also remember sensitive counseling with neighbors, a young Protestant woman who had signed a pledge to have her children raised in the Roman Catholic Church of her husband and was deeply troubled by the consequences now that blind love had passed. I also know of counseling sessions with parish priests when the effects of Vatican II were being felt at the local level. In his last full-time pastorate a delegation from the Roman Catholic parish asked him to consider being their priest, a request he felt was an honor even if it were most unlikely. At the least mother found being a housekeeper an odd designation for a wife of forty years.

When he and mother went to Burnley, England, to serve in an interim ministry for one year, they assisted in building an atmosphere which led in early 1987 to the Burnley Lane Fellowship of Churches: their Church of Christ, a Baptist Church, two Methodist Churches, two Churches of England and a Roman Catholic Church. Each was a small congregation much pressed by the secular culture of the English Midlands. In that setting these Christians found ways to work together, even on occasion to worship together as congregations with the Anglican and Roman Catholic bishops, the Baptist general superintendent, the Methodist district chairman, and the Church of Christ general secretary in attendance. The service involved a local covenant to which all subscribed.[9]

Years before that, as I neared graduation from Milligan College in Tennessee, Dad suggested I consider Westminster Theo-

9. The covenant reads: "We the people of Burnley Lane Baptist Church, the Church of Christ, New Hall Street, Colne Road Methodist Church, Elim Methodist Church, St. Andrew's Church of England, St. Cuthbert's Church of England, St. John the Baptist, Roman Catholic—repent of our past divisions which have hindered the proclamation of the Gospel;—confess our common faith in one God, our Creator, Sustainer and Saviour, made known to us by his Spirit in the person of Jesus and in the witness of Scripture;—acknowledge one another as members of the universal Church and as brothers and sisters in Christ;—recognize and rejoice in one another's traditions within the Christian faith, and respect the calls of obedience which they make upon us;—believe that we are called to display the oneness of God in the oneness of our life together so that all people may come to faith in God and in his Christ. As God grants us grace, we therefore covenant together to share our Christian pilgrimage, and to promote in whatever ways we can the visible unity and mission of the Church."

Set in the midst of a worship service, this covenant was signed by the "Church leaders and the Clergy and People of the local congregations covenanting together" and followed by the Lord's prayer.

logical Seminary in Philadelphia as one option. He had heard they were sound in the faith. (Had he read more about the narrow, fundamentalistic approach of the school, he would have had me rethink that option.) But I was in love and enrolled in a moderate to liberal seminary which gave me a full scholarship and my wife-to-be a half fellowship. First things first, my friends. In retrospect I now realize that while in seminary I nearly lost every smidgen of Christian faith I had. The farmer's faith in the cycles of life which had marked my father's experience and many of my summers had not left me, but much if not all of my faith in Christ had disappeared. The historical-critical study of Scripture led me to question everything it said. Most of the Bible appeared to be myth in the sense of something not much better than a comic book. In my second year of seminary study, while preaching at a small church in Oklahoma, I gave myself six months. If I could not find more to believe, for the sake of the congregation and my own integrity I should leave the ministry. It is amazing what you can do in such a period of struggle. You can preach parts of the ethical values found in Paul's letters without being much more than a good Stoic. And many conservative churches have heard such morality as the key subject for so long that they would neither be offended nor concerned for a few months. The Apostle Paul was much more than a Stoic, but at that period I was much less. Virgin birth, miracles, resurrection, and the second coming were worthy of Superman, but I was not certain they could be descriptive of anyone real. I wanted to give my life for others in some kind of service, but perhaps social services would be best. Yet in that period of little faith if not unfaith, two sets of things happened. First, the Kennedys and Martin Luther King, Jr., were killed. It wasn't so much the thought of my own death which bothered me as the clear sense that significant, serving humans could be eliminated from the struggle rather easily. Second, my mom wrote that dad had baptized a woman he met at the state prison, one who had been convicted of killing her little girl. When the woman was to be paroled, none of her family would take her. My parents did, even though my youngest sister was still in grade school. Where did they get the strength to do that? What wonderful social work.

When the six months were up, I could preach more from Paul

and much from Jesus. To reverse a famous Fundamentalist metaphor, I was on my way up the slippery slope. On the edges or perhaps outside the faith and struggling to do the honest thing for the congregation and myself, I came to know other viewpoints personally. When a Fundamentalist warns me of slippery slopes, of taking that one step down the incline which will cause you to slide into hell, I remember climbing step by step up out of "hell." As you will see in these chapters, I am very much a Christian who conserves the Tradition of Christ, but I feel freed by the gospel, as liberated as any liberal should be. I am concerned to hold on to the fundamentals of faith, but I seldom sense the need to battle for the Bible. Few if any would welcome me as a fellow Fundamentalist, but I know from home what Fundamentalists can be, both for good and ill. I am not properly identified as an Evangelical if it means that I must advocate the views of either Luther or Calvin or accept the great creedal tradition of the sixteenth century and the orthodoxy of the seventeenth, but I share much with certain of their number. The congregation in which I am actively involved is called a Christian Church and the best description of its tradition within Christianity is free-church catholic.[10] I prefer the simple, universal title "Christian" because I can make sense of what that means and am willing to accept that sense.[11]

10. At Lexington, Kentucky, in 1841, Alexander Campbell, one of the leaders of my heritage, the Christian Church, spoke for almost six hours on the following resolution: "That the union of Christians can be scripturally effected by requiring a practical acknowledgement of such articles of belief and such rules of piety and morality as are admitted by all Christian denominations." (A. Campbell, ed., *Millennial Harbinger,* 1841, 259). That resembles the Vincentian canon: what has been believed by everyone in every era in every place, and betrays no Protestant sectarian spirit. Campbell had debated Bishop Purcell of Cincinnati and contested the catholicity of Roman Catholicism in quite acrimonious terms. He retained that attitude toward official Roman Catholicism all of his life, but he knew only the Catholicism leading up to Vatican I. One of the best descriptions of my particular tradition is found in Alfred T. De Groot, *Disciple Thought: A History* (Fort Worth: Texas Christian University, 1965), who seems to have coined the phrase "free-church catholic."

11. As the term "evangelical" is often formulated, I am uncomfortable with it at a number of points. First, I prefer not to put evangelical and catholic in opposition. For me the gospel is basic to universal Christian Faith. Second, although late medieval western Christianity was in need of reform, I do not find the magisterial Reformation to be the best guide. From that period I prefer the Anabap-

tists' positions but reject the views of Thomas Muentzer and the Muenster rebellions. I am also impressed with the missionary activity of the Catholic Reformation. (Even Thomas Aquinas I find quite attractive because his theological efforts took place in the context of Christian mission to Islam.) My roots, however, are most deeply set in the New Testament and the Church fathers, particularly the Eastern ones. As a result I do not look much like a normal "evangelical" although the doctrine I hold dear is often important to Evangelicals.

# Part I
# Protestantism

# 1

# Fundamentalists and Evangelicals

Mainline Protestantism forms the foreground of any discussion of Fundamentalists and Evangelicals. The focus here, however, is on conservative Protestants. American Fundamentalism is a movement that began with my grandfather's generation but did not die with it. The *New Catholic Encyclopedia,* published in 1967, has a small article on fundamentalism which describes it as a phenomenon that was probably in permanent decline.[1] How we historians err as prophets. Although definitions are difficult, there are some that seem to fit both the results of study by historians and those who claim the name "fundamentalist" for themselves. Ed Dobson and Ed Hindson along with Jerry Falwell, the televangelist who started and wins support for Liberty University in Lynchburg, Virginia, are happy to be called Fundamentalists. They view George Marsden's definition as sympathetic and fair. He calls Fundamentalism "a twentieth-century movement closely tied to the revivalist tradition of mainstream evangelical Protestantism that militantly opposed modernist theology and the cultural change associated with it."[2] The Liberty University trio also claims

1. T. A. Collins, "Fundamentalism, Biblical," *New Catholic Encyclopedia* (New York: McGraw-Hill, 1967) 6:224.
2. Ed Dobson, Ed Hinson, Jerry Falwell, *The Fundamentalist Phenomenon: The Resurgence of Conservative Christianity,* 2nd ed. (Grand Rapids, Mich.: Baker Book House, 1986) 3, taken from Marsden, "Fundamentalism as an American Phenomenon: A Comparison with English Evangelicalism," *Church History* 46 (1977) 215. Marsden, *Fundamentalism and American Culture: The Shaping of Twentieth Century Evangelicalism (1870-1925)* (Oxford: Oxford University Press,

that five fundamentals, five specific doctrines, are basic to Fundamentalism, a position which Marsden also describes but with a bit different detail within the five points. For the Liberty University Fundamentalists they are: (1) The inspiration and infallibility of Scripture (2) The deity of Christ (including his virgin birth) (3) The substitutionary atonement of Christ's death (4) The literal resurrection of Christ from the dead (5) The literal return of Christ in the Second Advent.[3]

It is no accident that Marsden's description is taken seriously. He knows Fundamentalism from the inside and as a professional historian. His seminary degree was taken at Westminster in Philadelphia, one of the oldest fundamentalist institutions in this country. It was founded by B. B. Warfield and J. Gresham Machen when they lost the battle at Princeton and left to begin a new school for the education of ministers. Marsden has also gained recognition from scholars outside the fundamentalist camps. He did his doctoral work at Yale, won National Endowment for the Humanities support for his book *Fundamentalism and American Culture,* and now teaches at Notre Dame.

To expand on Marsden's definition, Fundamentalism is primarily a modern phenomenon, one located in the "twentieth century." The term seems to have been first coined by Curtis Lee Laws, the editor of an influential Northern Baptist periodical, *The Watchman Examiner,* in mid-1920.[4] It probably occurred to him because a series of twelve volumes called *The Fundamentals* had been published between 1910 and 1915 containing articles representing most if not all of the best minds among this conservative branch of Protestantism. In 1909 Lyman Stewart, a California millionaire, backed the idea and hired a noted evangelist, A. C. Dixon of the Moody Church in Chicago, to be the editor. By the time the twelfth volume appeared, Louis Meyer, a Jewish Christian evangelist, and then R. A. Torrey, an evangelist who had

1980) uses a similar description in his fuller treatment. Also see his "Defining American Fundamentalism," *The Fundamentalist Phenomenon: A View from Within; A Response from Without,* ed. Norman J. Cohen (Grand Rapids, Mich.: William B. Eerdmans, 1990) 22–37 and Clark Pinnock, "Defining American Fundamentalism: A Response," *The Fundamentalist Phenomenon,* 38–55.

3. Dobson, Hinson, Fallwell, *The Fundamentalist Phenomenon,* 2nd ed., 7–11.
4. Marsden, *Fundamentalism and American Culture,* 159.

graduated from Yale and studied in Germany, had also assumed editorial responsibilities. The authors, who came from both Great Britain and the United States, argued for what they considered to be the traditional Christian faith against the attacks of modernism. More than 300,000 copies were made available free to ministers and church leaders. Their impact was much more limited than those involved had hoped, but the project does mark the beginning of the movement.

The contributors clearly represented a "revivalist tradition," as Marsden says, in that all of the editors of *The Fundamentals* were themselves noted preachers. Many who wrote articles were also skilled pulpiteers. They were not all in agreement with the antics of a Billy Sunday, who, in the views of even some sympathetic observers, put on a circus with his virulent rhetoric and stage theatrics. Some of these conservatives could move people within a more sedate and dignified church service, not necessarily in tents or great auditoriums. They often could argue with almost impeccable logic in favor of what they considered to be the endangered doctrines of the Church. They might not have ranted and raved; some could reach the emotions of their hearers through the older, rhetorical insights of the classical Greek and Roman writers, in a manner somewhat similar to Jonathan Edwards' droning lectures. But move people they did.

The contemporary spate of televangelists of fundamentalist persuasion and notoriety (such as James Bakker, formerly of PTL, recently of prison, and Jimmy Swaggert) stand in a particular line with this revivalist tradition, more like Billy Sunday than Dwight L. Moody or the contemporary Billy Graham. They have progressed beyond radio to television with the same emotionally moving messages that marked many of the early fundamentalist leaders. There are any number of reasons for finding Bakker and Swaggert repulsive. Each apparently has had his own heterosexual escapades; perhaps one, bisexual experiences. Conservative Christians are not so taught and do not so believe. Both Bakker and Swaggert have had difficulty handling the financial wealth that came to them because of their success as television fundraisers; one has been convicted of misusing funds. Each has been willing to offend large sections of contemporary life with their singular claims for Christian truth. But they represent a genuine aspect of revivalist tradition although parts of it may be better understood by reading Sinclair Lewis' *Elmer Gantry* than by studying a biography of Billy Sunday.

There are other televangelists who are also outspoken Fundamentalists around whom a whole television culture has arisen. Pat Robertson's political career was short-lived, but fascinating. He, along with Jerry Falwell's Moral Majority, has demonstrated that these Fundamentalists have the clout to influence local elections—particularly in a country which now sees so few of its eligible voters go to the polls. Robertson's debacle and Falwell's withdrawal to Lynchburg in order to concentrate more on his university and the Thomas Road Baptist Church should not blind us to the power of revivalist, fundamentalist politics. A recent speaker at Falwell's Liberty University was Ollie North, proclaiming his patriotism and loyalty to American ideals in the face of congressional and foreign dangers to the constitution. Somehow his actions that led to a trial do not appear as moral failure or sin to his supporters.

Oral Roberts' star has faded; even his son seems unable to recover from the bizarre claims of his father's visions: both the positive dream of a fifty-foot Christ calling him to mission and the draconian God who demanded his life if he did not raise enough money to pay his debts. But at the same time these televangelists clearly—and often almost unrecognizably—give the lie to a charge that contemporary Fundamentalism is backward and totally antimodern. Who else has used the medium of television to extract so much money for their causes from the American public? By comparison the telethons for various diseases pale into oblivion.

According to Marsden's definition early Fundamentalists also came from "mainstream evangelical Protestantism." That went against the grain of most stereotypical portraits of Fundamentalists in the 1980s. Indeed many of the great pockets of fundamentalist strength appear to be on the fringes of Christiantiy both theologically and geographically. Snake handlers live primarily in Kentucky and Tennessee. Jerry Falwell claims a connection with Baptists and has located his center in Lynchburg, Virginia. Bob Jones University, a powerhouse of fundamentalist activity, is basically independent of "mainstream Protestantism" and is located in South Carolina. Perhaps the greatest theological school of

Fundamentalism—both in influence and in numbers—Dallas Theological Seminary with over 2,000 students, is in the Southwest. The stalwart seminary originally associated with Fundamentalism, Westminster in Philadelphia, is not directly associated with any mainline denomination.

The oddity involved in this contemporary look at Fundamentalism is that it was not originally so. Dayton, Tennessee, may have been the sight of its great debacle, the Scopes trial in which its momentum was blunted if not stopped, but at its inception American Fundamentalism battled in the mainstream. Its most impressive, early leaders and largest following were to be found among Northern Baptists and Northern Presbyterians. They themselves represented, both theologically and philosophically, a close relationship to the widespread and influential evangelical consensus that formed most of Protestantism in the mid-nineteenth century. Although Southern ministers in the nineteenth century were not as revivalistic as occasionally depicted,[5] they were not the strength of growing Fundamentalism. Respectable Baptists and Presbyterians in the North fought the early battles. The theological war followed a period when both the Divinity School of the University of Chicago, originally a Baptist school, and Union Theological Seminary in New York, originally a Presbyterian school, had been related to evangelical, mainstream Protestant heritages. In the early twentieth century they became dominated by other forces. The tremendous struggle at Princeton Theological Seminary was between the "Old School" conservatives and "New School" moderates. When Warfield and Machen left Princeton to form Westminster they were still Northern Presbyterians.

Philosophically Fundamentalism stood in a "mainstream" that had served "evangelical Protestantism" well but in the early twentieth century was either under attack or almost totally eclipsed by "modernist theology" and "cultural change." In the late eighteenth and early nineteenth centuries Common Sense Scottish philosophy had grown up in reaction to David Hume's radical skepticism. Hume did not find causation compelling. For him even hitting a cue ball into other billiard balls provided no clear example of cause and effect. Thus he consistently found claims of

---

5. E. Brooks Holifield, *The Gentlemen Theologians: American Theology in Southern Culture, 1795-1860* (Durham: Duke University Press, 1978).

resurrection or miracles to be illusory. Such things flew in the face of all probability. It was much more likely that this category of events was contrived than that it was real.

Hume's philosophical claims offended Scottish Presbyterianism and provided ground for the development of the Common Sense view. As simply put as possible, Thomas Reid, Dugald Stewart and others claimed that the mind directly perceived reality, that memory dealt with the facts, not mental pictures of those facts. In their view only philosophers questioned whether there was a real world to be known and real observers to know it. The bulk of humankind knew better than that, even if there were no way to demonstrate that those claims of objective reality and objective ways of knowing were true. As the professional theologians and general populace adopted forms of Common Sense philosophy, they did not emphasize the point that such objectivity was indemonstrable. They depended more and more on the "obvious" sense that a real world with objective observers was there.

The theological thrust of this philosophical position was tied to another strong assumption: all rational beings operated within this sense of objectivity. Eventually they would see the truth of Christian faith, indeed apprehend with clarity the absolute claims of evangelical Protestantism. Muslims and Roman Catholics could be led to the truth. The mainstream of evangelical Protestantism in early nineteenth-century America flowed swiftly through the banks of Common Sense philosophy. It was not concerned with Kant's critique of pure reason in which, to the satisfaction of many Europeans, he demonstrated that totally objective argument, particularly about religion, was impossible. He did not so much doubt the existence of a real world; he was deeply concerned with the subjective involvement of the observer in the process. That was the way in which he developed a response to Hume's skepticism. Again stated simply, Kant's sense of the observer's dilemma paved the way for the birth of classical liberalism in Germany, specifically in the person of Friedrich Schleiermacher, a concern more with personal religious experience than with general historical fact. Philosophically mainstream American evangelical Protestantism of the early and mid-nineteenth century did not share what came to be the great European tradition every seminary student is now called upon to learn.

There was, however, a steady trickle of bright theological students to European, particularly German, universities, in the mid- to late nineteenth century, who did learn this tradition. Indeed scientific theories such as evolution, an English Darwinism, were investigated within scholarly circles in this country. Intellectually some of the "ancient truths" of Christian faith were directly challenged not only at a philosophical and epistemological level, but on the basis of direct observation of real phenomena. What to do with the dinosaur bones? Did some giant dog bury them in selected backyards? If they were not colossal hoaxes, where did they fit in the scheme of things? The great intellectual heritage of nineteenth-century evangelical Protestantism was not prepared for these philosophical and scientific changes although in a way not usually acknowledged, it did not see these developments as cause for a war between science and religion.[6]

At the same time, recovery from the devastation of the American Civil War, the continued industrialization of the country with its dislocation of people, wealth, and power, and the dreariness of World War I, could be confronted from within at least three strong options. Some Americans were disillusioned with the constantly shifting demands of life and found religion no resource at all. Others were drawn to a modernistic approach that radically adjusted the faith according to the new discoveries within all disciplines of human understanding. Still others, many in the South, recovered from the desolation through strengthened ties to conservative, experientially satisfying, revivalistic religion. But especially in the industrialized North, there were individuals and families who looked for something immovable. Immigrant families with strong ties to Catholicism in Europe continued their active participation in parishes within this country. Among Protestants the philosophically objectivist, doctrinally traditional and emotionally satisfying churches grew at phenomenal rates.

Yet cracks began to occur. Most importantly as the growth of churches decreased at the beginning of the twentieth century, it

6. David N. Livingstone, *Darwin's Forgotten Defenders: The Encounter Between Evangelical Theology and Evolutionary Thought* (Grand Rapids, Mich:. William B. Eerdmans, 1987). The early battle was scientist against scientist. A number of important evangelical theologians did not oppose the Darwinian hypothesis.

became clear that something was wrong with the objectivist approach. If all people who were rational could indeed accept the facts and believe, why, as modern life unfolded, did so many not do so? Some staunch Calvinists could follow Augustine into a type of predestination in which people's refusal to believe was attributed to their sinfulness and submerged in the mysterious majesty of God's predestining plan. But some American evangelical Protestants, although not optimistic about human nature, were more attuned to Arminianism in their views of human nature. They thought that average folks had the intellect and the will to respond to the gospel. Why didn't they?

Within the circles that spawned Fundamentalism, both intellectually alert and more pragmatically awake, these questions were nagging but usually answered with a tighter apologetic among some and a more emotional appeal among others. On the one hand, the "Old School" Princetonians like Warfield and Machen made their contributions with magnificent, logical studies of the problems presented by theological modernism or Liberalism and the contemporary cultural changes. Doctrines should not be adjusted to meet contemporary standards; they should be defended vigorously on the basis of the facts. Liberal science was not scientific and liberal history was not historical. The wrong presuppositions about knowledge and ways of knowing ruined the objectivity of real life, threatened it with a subjectivity that could destroy everything. These early fundamentalist leaders did not see American culture as marked by the deep pessimism that conquered much of Europe after World War I, but they did see it as endangered by a basic subjectivity that destroyed real facts in any area of knowledge.

On the other hand, revivals continued with a deeper sense of urgency. How could the lost be reached? What methods, what illustrations, what styles of preaching and testimonies moved them? The assumption again was that in spite of the great Augustinian tradition, hearers could respond. Within some aspects of that tradition, the Spirit could and did move to give prevenient grace to those in need. Revivalists have struggled to find such a way well into the present era.

I have left the striking verb of Marsden's definition until now. According to him Fundamentalists "militantly opposed" their enemies.[7] The Modernist-Fundamentalist struggle was a war. Early on they battled within the mainstream denominations for positions of authority and control of the purse strings. It is difficult at times to see which side was the more bitter and irrational. During World War I, classical Liberals at the Divinity School of the University of Chicago even accused the Fundamentalists of being supported by German financial interests that were attempting to sabotage the war effort. Clearly some Fundamentalists were pacifists. The hysteria of wartime often makes fools of us all and makes killing seem honorable. It is, however, at best ironic, at worst ludicrous, to think of those great Chicago liberals as warmongers attacking pacifism. What freedom. What liberality.

Within the early 1920s Fundamentalists had much success both through the instrument of heresy trials and general financial or personal pressure. From 1920–1925 they seemed to have tremendous momentum. But they also suffered deep losses. The plethora of Bible institutes and Bible colleges often came from defeats and withdrawals from the more normal nineteenth-century educational processes for ministry. Some of these new institutions were marked by a nearly complete abandonment of study in the liberal arts and the sciences, a precursor of the contemporary attacks on "humanism" and "scientism." Others, following the model of the "Old School" Presbyterians, demanded an immersion in the classical Western heritage so that the "unfounded" claims to logical, historical, and scientific learning made by the Modernists could be attacked.

Much of Fundamentalism became after 1925 culturally gun-shy and separatist. Its institutions withdrew from the major streams of intellectual life and began to set up their own canons of truth over against the liberal attack on Scripture. They knew that they must be able to hold out for the Lord in the midst of these Philistines. Others, however, such as the founders of Fuller

---

7. Marsden, "Fundamentalism as an American Phenomenon: A Comparison with English Evangelicalism," *Church History* 46 (1977) 215 says immediately following his compact definition: "Fundamentalism shares traits with many other movements to which it has been related (such as pietism, evangelicalism, revivalism, conservatism, confessionalism, millenarianism, and the holiness and pentecostal movements), but it has been distinguished most clearly from these by its militancy in opposition to modernism."

Seminary in Pasadena, California, intended from the beginning to save Western culture another way. They knew that they were in a battle for the Bible, but along with it they were in a war over the survival of Christendom's great cultural achievements.[8] If they lost, darkness, unparalleled—in their view—even by the creeping shadows of medieval Romanism, would cover the globe. This apparent megalomania had much truth to it provided their presuppositions were granted. If the war was not only about revelation and inspiration but also about the content of knowledge and how it was obtained, their defeat would result in the death of Western culture that depended so much on Christianity.

The contest was between the forces of darkness and the forces of light. Apocalyptic features of Biblical texts were appropriated with regularity. Who is on the Lord's side? With these clearly perceived stakes, it was difficult to talk of love or even tolerance. Many could not. More often than any historian lacking the necessary empathy can understand, deep frustrations moved participants almost to despair. Personalities that despised conflict and looked for ways of bridging over the gaps were pilloried by both sides. Odd coalitions emerged. In one instance, both somewhat liberal and arch-conservative leaders among Northern Baptists claimed that the Scriptures were sufficient as a test of faith and practice. That position infuriated Fundamentalists who were ready to introduce a strict creed to make the Liberals choose traditional faith or membership within the Northern Baptists' fellowship.

Among both Modernists and Fundamentalists, being a battle-scarred veteran, a steely-nerved combatant whether with logical acuity or emotional passion, was honored. Fight. If you lose, withdraw to fight again. If you must separate from a denomination, or culture, or anything else, remain pure and fight. As the Fundamentalists lost in the late 1920s and 1930s, they often separated.

---

8. Carl F. H. Henry, *Twilight of a Great Civilization: The Drift Toward Neo-Paganism* (Westchester, Ill.: Crossway Books, 1988), primarily reprints essays from 1986–1988, but the volume opens with "The Barbarians Are Coming," reprinted from 1970. Also see ch. IV, "Rebuilding Western Civilization," of Marsden's *Reforming Fundamentalism: Fuller Seminary and the New Evangelicalism* (Grand Rapids, Mich.: William B. Eerdmans, 1987) 69–82 for a view of how important this theme was to the early vision of Fuller Seminary.

But in that combat Liberals who also could handle an axe were the chosen among their compatriots. They too were defending the truth of Christianity and the heritage of Western culture. Fighting for freedom and toleration was common.[9]

As most of the Fundamentalists retreated from the field, apparently to disappear as the *New Catholic Encyclopedia* writer predicted, the fighting spirit persisted among many of them. They were regrouping for a more favorable skirmish. The Modernists or Liberals, who in most instances kept either access to or control of the various institutions: presbyteries, conferences, mission stations, seminaries, colleges, universities, etc., became tolerant and sometimes condescending, perhaps more because they had won than because they were essentially loving. The suffering of fools, defined by winners, has never been a wide-spread virtue even though it is a politically sound strategy.

In the midst of Fundamentalism's retreat various pressures were changing its forces. Separatism from culture and rebellious allies became a mark of fidelity. Figures like Carl McIntire of Westminster Theological Seminary cast an eagle's eye on all who were acknowledged enemies and those who might have defected. His periodical often ran front-page articles decrying some apparently faithful Fundamentalist who had gone over to the other side. Simply naming someone as belonging to the enemy was more important than presenting his or her arguments and combatting them. (Those of us watching recent presidential races know how effective that method still is.) McIntire's energies were vented on the developing Fuller Theological Seminary, the home of contemporary Evangelicalism.

In the present era "Evangelicalism" or "Neo-Evangelicalism," so-called by its supporters and detractors alike, has deep American roots in the Fundamentalist heritage of the twentieth century

9. In the contemporary period the effects of these kinds of battles can be seen in the work of James Barr, *Fundamentalism* (Philadelphia: Westminster Press, 1977), which concentrates on Protestant Fundamentalists and that of Thomas F. O'Meara, *Fundamentalism: A Catholic Perspective* (New York: Paulist Press, 1990), which focuses on the larger phenomena but is particularly interested in Catholic Fundamentalism. Both books are marked by considerable irritation and anger. Having dealt with ardent Fundamentalists I can understand those reactions. But they tend to weaken both books, particularly Barr's.

and the evangelical Protestant traditions of the nineteenth century. Billy Graham has picked up the mantle of Billy Sunday and Dwight L. Moody and put into practice their evangelistic revivals. His crusades, early backed by such unlikely supporters as the Hearst newspapers, began to attract thousands. Faithful to the Five Fundamentals, Graham developed a loving and pragmatic spirit that was tolerant of many different views within Christianity. He went beyond the image of a heroic warrior. He adapted to radio, then television and film to become one of the televangelists who did not indulge in the pleasures of sexual arousal and financial power that his position doubtless allowed. He even created institutional structures to guard against such problems. Never moving his crusades from the preaching and singing format of the earlier revivalists—no talkshow or entertainment formats— he has a relatively high profile among most Americans, one above the present ridicule of televangelists. He can be sharp in his descriptions and rebuke of sin, but he does not strike one as primarily a fighter and a separatist. His political involvements were strong during the Nixon administration and now, although much more publicly subdued, are still significant. He was the religious leader standing by George Bush during the final decision for war in the Middle East. As an Evangelical he has been influential in the development of certain evangelical institutions, particularly Wheaton College and Fuller Theological Seminary.

In many ways the history of Fuller in Pasadena, California offers the clearest example of the new evangelical developments.[10] While there are indications that some of the new Evangelicals carry the burden of battle-planning, most of them stand within a more moderating spirit. They can argue strongly against some of the philosophical and cultural errors they see in contemporary culture, but they tend to gravitate toward involvement with scholarly and denominational institutions. Most Evangelicals are not separatists. They emphasize scholarly credentials from great universities; they seek to penetrate denominations through proper channels. Often the inheritors of separatist institutions set up by Fundamentalists of a prior era, they have sought accreditation

10. Marsden was asked by Fuller's president, David Hubbard, to write the account and was given access to the school's records. See his *Reforming Fundamentalism,* vii–ix.

of their colleges not only by the Association of Bible Colleges but also by regional accrediting agencies that oversee even state universities. Their success has been so strong that a number of Bible colleges and institutes of fundamentalist persuasion have begun to follow their example. The faculties in their educational institutions often have attained their highest degrees from world-class universities. There are still certain prejudices against them among the educational establishment because they become identified with Fundamentalists or are denied "true" academic status because they have firm commitments to the truth of Christian faith.

They have developed remarkable philosophical prowess even to the point of offering new options to the Common Sense approach to reality. The work of the Calvin College philosophers, Nicholas Wolterstorff who now teaches at Yale and Alvin Plantinga who now teaches at Notre Dame,[11] has emphasized the confessional, non-foundational character of the response to David Hume with the result that the subjective involvement of the observer is accounted for without a collapse into solipsism. Descartes' search for that one foundation upon which all else can be based has been abandoned. Developments of personalism in physics and the collapse of logical positivism have been incorporated into a view that does not deny the existence of facts, but also recognizes the unavoidable subjectivism of the observer. The Heisenberg principle, obviously a modern position, has been accounted for in this epistemology. Whatever the observer looks at, hears, or touches is in some way affected by that observer's presence. Certainly observers' descriptions of events are colored by their views. Thus all should admit their commitments at the beginning; none should be shy about having them. This Evangelical development clearly shows how some Evangelicals are in the center of modern scholarly debate.

Yet some definitions of Evangelicalism are notoriously deficient because they trace the stream of its development back through Old School Presbyterianism with a nod to the revival-

11. Nicholas Wolterstorff, *Reason within the Bounds of Religion,* 2nd ed. (Grand Rapids, Mich.: William B. Eerdmans, 1984). Nicholas Wolterstorff and Alvin Plantinga, *Faith and Rationality: Reason and Belief in God* (Notre Dame, Ind.: University of Notre Dame Press, 1983). Wolterstorff has recently been chosen to give the prestigious Gifford Lectures in Scotland.

ism of Billy Sunday and Dwight L. Moody. The contemporary National Association of Evangelicals, the largest group in the United States, includes not only the inheritors of Old School Presbyterianism but also a large block of so-called Pentecostal and Holiness groups. Although exact counts are difficult to attain it is probable that over half and up to two-thirds of the members of NAE come from Pentecostal and Holiness traditions. Thus the continued emphasis upon propositional revelation and doctrinal precision which marks many descriptions of Evangelicals is itself skewed. Although the Pentecostal and Holiness heritages have never been without doctrinal positions, they are often every bit as much interested in personal and communal experience as well as ethical life. And more often than not they are the engines which drive conservative Protestantism in the United States. No explanation of Protestant Evangelicals can begin to be acceptable if it does not indicate how important these groups are.[12]

To summarize then, Fundamentalists, as Marsden says, are "a twentieth-century movement closely tied to the revivalist tradition of mainstream evangelical Protestantism that militantly opposed modernist theology and the cultural change associated with it." Evangelicals share much of that heritage although they may be more influenced by the revivalist stream particularly as it is seen in Pentecostal and Holiness traditions. As a rule they are also less "militantly" opposed to things modern. Theologically, Evangelicals are very close to Fundamentalists if one examines the five fundamentals. That is why they are often mistaken for Fundamentalists. Although their interests are much broader and

12. Donald W. Dayton, *Theological Roots of Pentecostalism* (Grand Rapids, Mich.: Francis Asbury Press of Zondervan Publishing, 1987) clearly details what the title proposes so that Pentecostalism cannot be dismissed as theologically naive. His article, "Yet Another Layer of the Onion, or Opening the Ecumenical Door to Let the Riffraff in," *The Ecumenical Review* 40 (1988) 87–110 shows how often historical sketches of Fundamentalism and Evangelicalism as well as descriptions of the contemporary phenomena do not even know about much of the primary literature and describe both movements with little or no attention to pentecostal and holiness aspects. The results for such issues as the place of women and social ethics is utterly disastrous. Pentecostal and Holiness groups recognized women ministers from their beginnings and often were leaders in causes such as the abolition of slavery. Oberlin College, originally a holiness institution, was the first to recruit and graduate African-American women.

their spirit more irenic most Evangelicals support the four positions about Christ: his deity including the virgin birth, his substitutionary atonement, his resurrection and second coming. Those points, however, can be best discussed in our fourth chapter on Jesus Christ. The fifth point, the inerrancy of the Bible, is hotly debated within Evangelical circles. But that debate is the focus of the next chapter.

# 2

# Scripture and Tradition

Television, not the least Bill Moyers with his Texas Baptist roots, has given us rather insightful coverage of the struggle among Southern Baptists in which Fundamentalists have insisted on the inerrancy of Scripture as *the* test of orthodoxy. Since 1979 Southern Baptist Fundamentalists have sought to rid that denomination of any leaders who do not confess that the Bible is the errorless Word of God. On the other side, moderates defend the Baptist heritage that supports the freedom of individual conscience and the rejection of creeds as tests of fellowship. Although as a whole Southern Baptists are conservative Protestants, the moderate wing has been taking a beating as "liberal" whenever they do not insist on biblical inerrancy.[1]

This battle is strange for any who do not have much contact with Protestantism, and little or none with evangelical or fundamentalist Protestantism. For here are Baptists who overwhelmingly support four of the five positions that Fundamentalists staked out—the deity of Christ, his substitutionary atonement, his resurrection from the dead, and his second coming—fighting about the first claim. Thus there are very few, if any, classical Liberals among Southern Baptists. And all Baptists known to me preach the importance of a life of holiness. Yet they are bitterly

1. See Alan Neely, "Southern Baptists' Quiet Conflict: The 1980s Fundamentalist Drive and Its Aftermath," *Christianity and Crisis* 50 (March 5, 1990) 61–65. The election of a fundamentalist leader in their most recent convention has almost guaranteed that their great institutions for ministerial education, including Southern Baptist Theological Seminary in Louisville, will be purged of moderates.

divided over the first of the fundamentals: inerrancy. Fundamentalists espouse the literal inerrancy of Scripture and often attack historical, critical study of the Bible as it has developed since the Enlightenment. Evangelicals vary in their approach to the inerrancy of Scripture and often accept, with significant modifications, the historical, critical study of the Bible. The debate within Southern Baptist Churches pits Fundamentalists against Evangelicals concerning the doctrine of inerrancy.

What is that doctrine? Inerrancy, in its strongest sense, means that there are no errors of any kind in Scripture. Although to many people biblical inerrancy seems to be a new teaching, it is not. Both Fundamentalists and Evangelicals who support it find its foundations directly in Scripture. They build their case on what they see as clear biblical texts that speak about the inspiration of Scripture. I mention only three of the most prominent passages, all taken from the New Testament.

The first is John 10:34-36. From the Revised Standard Version it reads: "Jesus answered them, 'Is it not written in your law, "I said, you are gods."'? If he called them gods to whom the word of God came (and scripture cannot be broken), do you say of him whom the Father consecrated and sent into the world, "You are blaspheming," because I said "I am the Son of God."' "

In these verses "Word of God" and "Scripture" are treated as synonymous. When Jesus himself speaks about the Word of God and Scripture in the same breath, how could a Christian do otherwise? As importantly, Jesus not only quotes Scripture authoritatively as the Word of God; he also insists that it "cannot be broken." It would be busted if it had errors. According to the defender of biblical inerrancy, these simple statements, definitions, and synonyms are clear. Most importantly, the divine Son of God himself says the Bible is inerrant.

Furthermore, this text can function in a strange way within a Fundamentalist's attack on historical critical study of Scripture. In that immortal phrase from the heartland, "If it ain't broke, don't fix it." Why fiddle around with Scripture when it ain't broke? It just says what it means, and means what it says. Although many sophisticated people wince at the principle stated in such a downhome way, some of them are also puzzled by the remarkable ways in which they hear Scripture explained as not saying what it apparently says. You do not have to live in the South and have an eighth-grade education to find some interpretations baffling.

The second text, foundational for this view, is 2 Peter 1:19-21. These verses read: "And we have the prophetic word made more sure. You will do well to pay attention to this as a lamp shining in a dark place, until the day dawns and the morning star rises in your hearts. First of all you must understand this, that no prophecy of Scripture is a matter of one's own interpretation, because no prophecy ever came by the impulse of man, but men moved by the Holy Spirit spoke from God."

Here the important contrast, according to an inerrantist, is between human factors and the Word of God. Biblical prophecy never came from human impulses whether those impulses were founded in religious genius and insight or in unusual personal experience. Humans are not the authors of Scripture; God is. People were moved by the Holy Spirit and spoke words from God. Again this apparently clear interpretation rests on a distinction that is logically drawn. Either a human or God is the ultimate source of any biblical text. These verses reject human impulse and teach God's authorship. If Scripture is a word from the Lord, if its author is God, then it must be perfect, for God is perfect. Furthermore this argument has special weight because many supporting inerrancy would see the apostle Peter as its human scribe.

The point is not without force. When in the history of Christianity has Holy Scripture been viewed universally as only the words of humans? For many Christians who do not see themselves as Protestant Fundamentalists or Evangelicals, a Bible put forth as totally human, full of old wives' tales and fiction, is not the Bible used within their churches. In recent literature one Roman Catholic lawyer has claimed the inerrancy of Scripture as something he, other conservative Catholics and conservative Protestants share.[2]

The third, 2 Timothy 3:14-16, reads as follows: "But as for

2. William Bentley Ball, "Why Can't We Work Together," *Christianity Today* 34 (July 16, 1990) 23. *Christianity Today* is probably the most influential conservative Protestant magazine in the United States. Ball had published a similar appeal "We'd Better Hang Together: It's Time for a New Alliance Between Catholics and Evangelicals" in a Roman Catholic journal, *Crisis* (October, 1989) 17-21.

you, continue in what you have learned and firmly believed, knowing from whom you learned it and how from childhood you have
been acquainted with the sacred writings which are able to instruct
you for salvation through faith in Christ Jesus. All scripture is
inspired by God and profitable for teaching, for reproof, for cor-
rection, and for training in righteousness, that the man of God
may be complete, equipped for every good work."

From these verses a supporter of biblical inerrancy emphasizes
the Greek word behind the English phrase "inspired by God,"
that is, *theopneustos.* If Scripture is literally "God-breathed,"
and God is without error, then Scripture cannot contain error.
According to this logic, to say that the Bible is not correct in its
details, one must deny either that the Bible is "God-breathed,"
or that God is without error. The simplicity and force of that argument are easily seen. Again according to inerrantists the syllogisms behind it come directly from an apostolic author, this time
Paul.

Yet there are problems with these apparently literal interpretations. It is not clear from John 10:34-36 that Scripture's inability
to be broken must mean that it is errorless. The phrase, "scripture cannot be broken" is an aside within the text, one which has
little to do with the flow of its thought. It can only mean that
the Bible is inerrant if the reader injects a systematic theology that
supplies synonyms or inferences for the actual words in the text.
The interpretation, placed on the poetic language as the singular
meaning of its statements, restricts its meaning. That "scripture
cannot be broken" can speak more of the trustworthiness, the
power of God in his biblical word, the eternal character of its
truths, rather than the sense that there are no problems with any
scriptural texts. A Christian with a high view of Scripture, one
who takes the Bible as *the* authority in Christianity, need not make
unbrokenness synonymous with inerrancy.

A similar critique confronts the interpretation of 2 Peter
1:20-21. The concept of error which inerrantists find in this passage is actually based on an inference. The text emphasizes the
difference between human impulse and being moved by the Spirit
to speak from God, but it does not mention error. Again a concept or word has been introduced as synonymous with what the
verses actually say, almost as if Alexander Pope's lines: "To err

is human, to forgive divine" were part of a Bible dictionary with a significant change in the last line: "To err is human, to be inerrant divine."

2 Timothy 3:16 has no copula, no "is." We do not know if the emphasis should be that "All scripture *is* inspired by God," or that "All scripture, inspired by God, *is* profitable. . . . " In either case this verse teaches that Scripture is inspired, but the second translation would refer to the difficulty people in the earliest Christian communities were having in recognizing which writings were Scripture. Inspired Scripture at least met the criterion of being writings profitable for Christian virtue. If this interpretation be true, then the claim to inspiration itself was not sufficient to mark a book as Scripture. No Jew would doubt that Scripture was inspired; but the question would be, which books are Scripture? We know that early Christian writings other than those in the New Testament claimed inspiration and that Gnostic gospels often claimed to be written by apostles. It was not easy for an early Christian congregation to recognize which books belonged to Christian Scripture.

2 Timothy 3:16 does not say that "God-breathed" means "errorless." At times some Fundamentalists have defended a dictation view of inspiration: God gave the Scripture-writers both thoughts and words in a manic takeover of all their faculties. They wrote while in God-inspired trances. Philo, the great Hellenistic Jewish interpreter of the Old Testament who lived in Alexandria, Egypt, and died about 50 C.E., defined inspiration that way. But in the twentieth century both fundamentalist and evangelical proponents of biblical inerrancy usually reject that teaching. They do not think that inspiration blotted out all human consciousness among the writers. For them, however, it does mean that God protected their writings from error.

Notice that the biblical text itself uses the rather picturesque and poetic "God-breathed" while the defenders of inerrancy make the word synonymous with being free from error. That is an interpretation, a logical inference which may not follow. As a colleague of mine used to say, "I believe everything the Bible says about inerrancy." Since Scripture never uses the word, that well might be a show-stopper. Does every Christian have to accept "inerrancy" as synonymous with "God-breathed" in order to view the Bible as the inspired word of God? I think not. In fact, Scripture may be taken with more seriousness when it is not viewed as inerrant.

Within the full context of the 2 Timothy 3 passage, one other aspect is seldom acknowledged by fundamentalist or evangelical inerrantists. The writer of the letter, usually assumed by conservative Protestants to be the apostle Paul, calls Timothy to remember the people from whom he had heard the Word of God, those who had taught it to him. The Word of God is Tradition handed down in community; it is not learned alone. Timothy was to remember particularly the beloved women of his immediate family, his grandmother Lois, his mother Eunice and probably others. Paul did not tell Timothy to go into a closet and read Scripture by himself. This passage directly opposes an individualistic interpretation of the Bible; it keeps Scripture within the community of the faithful.

A more general criticism can be raised against inerrantists' uses of these texts. The meanings they find within them come from a particular schematic imposed on the passages. Their selection of these verses is based upon a specific sense of revelation as propositional. Simply put, it means that the truth of God's revelation depends upon whether or not its meaning can be translated into proper logical form and tested to see if it is valid. You may remember the old syllogism of three propositions from a logic book: "All Men are Mortal; Socrates is a Man; Therefore Socrates is Mortal." Supporters of biblical inerrancy usually see this use of propositions as the only or at least the primary way in which truth can be determined. Thus they translate the more poetic images in these biblical texts about Scripture into quasi-logical propositions. "Scripture cannot be broken; To be broken is to be in error; Therefore Scripture cannot be in error." The interpretation of these three texts from John, 2 Peter, and 2 Timothy depends on such syllogisms and thus the exact synonymous correlation of "God-breathed" with "inerrant" and a prophecy from God—as opposed to an impulse from man—with infallibility.

That kind of interpretation raises a significant question. If revelation must be in a syllogistically propositional form to be truthful, if the truth of Scripture can only be tested in such a specific, logical manner, if each sentence or phrase must be fit within a tight system, why does Scripture have the many forms it does? Most children are introduced to the content of Christian faith through biblical stories. Scripture is full of such wonderful narratives and anecdotes. Sometimes they are constructed for the purpose, as in Jesus' parable of the prodigal son. Sometimes they are historical narratives that run from chronicles of deeds done by kings to something as unusual and yet treated historically as miracles and indeed resurrection itself.

The insistence on the form of logical propositions alone as the way in which truth claims must be made and the failure to take the many forms of Scripture seriously is always puzzling to me. Fundamentalists and certain Evangelicals often fight against the historical-critical study of Scripture with a vengeance when that scholarship works with what is called form criticism. Form criticism is the investigation of the linguistic forms used to express things in the Bible: parable, preaching, poetry, wisdom sayings, historical narrative, etc. Certain conservative Protestants, with some justification, have called attention to the assumptions of the biblical interpreters who use form criticism. Does early Christian preaching so fit the needs of the community that the content of that preaching has no historical reliability? Although the arguments these conservatives make are sometimes unsound, they do raise legitimate questions concerning the relationship of linguistic form and truth. Yet oddly these Fundamentalists or Evangelicals too often see no danger whatsoever in transforming Scripture into the form of logical propositions, because, as they either presuppose or say specifically, no other form but logical propositions can be used to decide if something is true.

If that assumption is correct, that is, nothing but logical propositions usually arranged in syllogisms can be employed to test the truthfulness of biblical content, why didn't God know that? According to this view of an inerrantist, God, as the author of Scripture, put what he wanted to say in the forms of historical narrative, poetry, parable, wisdom sayings, letters, apocalypses, and only occasionally in the form of logical propositions. Why did he do that? Did he make a dreadful mistake?

As I see it, the claim that revelation must be in logical propositions itself interjects error into God's plan. In this view the selection of particular biblical texts and the transformation of those verses into propositions is to be the theologian's task. He or she corrects God's lack of attention to form. Had God known better he would have used the proper propositional forms and saved all of us much pain in translating biblical texts into syllogisms. My question is a simple one. If it is conservative to battle against the "perversion" of the Bible by form critics who change much of what Scripture appears to say, why is it conservative to insist the truth of Scripture only appears when its form is changed into logical propositions?

As a student of early Christianity I am struck by this anomaly in the following ways. Aetius and Eunomius, the two best known leaders among the later Arians in the fourth century C.E., taught that the Son was subordinate to the Father, even of a different divine nature. Roman Catholics find the view that Christ was less than fully God heretical; Fundamentalists and Evangelicals agree. But the Cappadocian Fathers who combatted the later Arians insisted that the struggle take place on levels other than the content of the creed. They also demanded that Aetius' and Eunomius' method of transforming the faith into a strict system of logical propositions be abandoned. That method of applying tightly formed syllogisms distorted the whole gospel. Even after a revelation sufficient and clear enough for our salvation, God is still beyond us. God's deepest nature is incomprehensible. That gulf demands that God cajole us, that God tell us, in the sharpest condescension one can imagine—without being condescending—who God is and what God wants. Thus God tries to persuade us with every means available: historical narrative, poetry, parables, wisdom sayings, apocalyptic, logical argument, etc. Theology as humans do it must then be reflections on revelation, a kind of probability science, that can never be demonstrative in the toughest, logical way. Theology need not be irrational or illogical. You don't need to be stupid to be a Christian; it may not even help. But in the end faith will give fullness to reasoning, rather than reasoning providing the foundation for faith.[3]

3. See *Faith Gives Fullness to Reasoning: The Five Theological Orations of Gregory Nazianzen,* intro. and comm. by Frederick W. Norris, trans. by Lionel Wickham and Frederick Williams (Leiden, E. J. Brill, 1991).

In some ways modern Fundamentalists and Evangelicals, who support inerrancy, defend orthodoxy through means used by arch-heretics. They are convinced of the essential function of logical propositions for any conception of truth, and thus consistently miss the ways in which truth appears in forms other than syllogisms. Again as simply as I know how to put it, you seldom can get to know people, to understand who they are or to recognize their character, by forming syllogisms about them. You live around them and watch. You listen to their stories and stories told about them. The introduction of this book included tales of my grandfather and father because it seemed the best way to tell you what Fundamentalism and Evangelicalism are and who I am. If Christian revelation appears ultimately in the incarnate Christ, a person, and arrives penultimately through prophets and apostles, persons who spoke and wrote, we should expect the forms we find in Scripture. That does not mean history or parable or poetry is untrue. It means that the inerrantist's sense of the truth is too limited. For the sake of understanding the Bible, inerrantists transform Scripture and then choose a medium that itself is questionable, if not heretical, as the ultimate form for Christian doctrine. Indeed much of conservative Protestant theology still depends upon a kind of foundationalism which insists that there must be an unassailable basis for all legitimate claims. Descartes becomes the hidden author, the one who supplies the great assumption. With the collapse of that foundationalism,[4] the very employment of terms like "inerrancy" for any phenomenon becomes not only suspect but unintelligible.

Another set of observations is in order. Scripture writers do not always speak of themselves as if their words were unbroken or God-breathed in the sense of being errorless. Writers of the psalms confess that the knowledge of God is too wonderful, too

---

4. Again see Stephen Toulmin, *Cosmopolis* (New York: The Free Press, 1990) and Ronald Thiemann, "Radiance and Obscurity in Biblical Narrative," *Scriptural Authority and Narrative Interpretation,* ed. Garrett Green (Philadelphia: Fortress Press, 1987) 26 and n. 12. Kathleen C. Boone, *The Bible Tells Them So: The Discourse of Protestant Fundamentalism* (Albany, N.Y.: The State University of New York Press, 1989) reaches similar conclusions not so much from standard philosophical sources as from literary ones like the work of Michel Foucault, E.D. Hirsch, Stanley Fish, and Edward Said. Her analysis is accurate and original.

high for them to attain it. Job and Daniel confess that they at times uttered things that were beyond their understanding. Paul carefully distinguishes between his own opinions—still in Scripture—and things that he considers teachings from the Lord. Although this is not the place to rehearse the data, there are numerous passages in which details do not agree. As an historian that does not surprise me. I never deal with any incidents that are described in exactly the same way by my sources. In fact if an historian confronts descriptions of an event that seem to come from different witnesses yet have exactly the same details in every case, the historian suspects collusion. So do the police and judges. The event probably did not occur as described; the witnesses who claim to have seen it probably lied or at least fudged a bit. If the inerrantists were to reach their goal, if Scripture did have every detail in perfect agreement with every other detail, it would be suspect from beginning to end—at least according to historical and judicial canons that are quite important to inerrantists. Once again, the Bible as it stands with some details not exactly the same has a better chance of being taken seriously than an "inerrant" Scripture would.

To give these conservative interpreters their due, however, the attacks of classical Liberals on the accuracy of the Bible in the late nineteenth and early twentieth centuries were too often grossly overdone. There was a kind of nitpicking, or as Scripture might put it, a choking on gnats and a swallowing of camels. As an historian of things ancient, I can say that the biblical texts are more reliable than other literature from the ancient world. They present problems, indeed significant ones at points, but in many ways they are rather remarkable. I constantly rely on textual evidence based in ninth- and tenth-century C.E. Byzantine Greek texts to sketch the positions taken by a fourth-century B.C.E. figure like Aristotle. Books on Aristotle do not begin customarily with the suggestion that extreme caution must be used in claiming to know what Aristotle said or wrote because over thirteen hundred years separate our full texts from the writer himself. They just say, "Aristotle says." When I mention Irenaeus' work, *The Demonstration of the Apostolic Preaching,* a Christian text written in the second century C.E., I often think about the fact that all we have is one manuscript copy of an Armenian translation of this

Greek work. How will we know if the translator got it right? We can look at the Greek of some of Irenaeus' other pieces or the Latin translation of other sections of his writings. But in the end what do you know when you check an Armenian translation with a Latin translation of a different lost Greek work by the same author? By comparison we have overwhelming manuscript evidence for most biblical books, particularly the New Testament. As a student of the fathers I seldom if ever work with textual evidence as sound as that available to students of the New Testament.

Yet one warning must also be sounded here. The manuscript evidence for New Testament books is astoundingly good when compared to other texts from their era and regions. Yet there are textual problems that are not easily solved, ones that leave us unclear about what a specific text actually says. Although their number is relatively small, they are not theologically insignificant. And there are centuries between the manuscripts of the Old Testament and the origin of their contents. Thus on the one hand we must speak of Scripture's textual reliability while on the other hand we recognize the continuing problems.

Protestant inerrantists do not base their views on Scripture and logic alone. Many of them have insisted that the great Tradition of the Church has claimed that Scripture is inerrant. They start with lists of the fathers and even end at times with statements from the Roman Catholic Council, Vatican I. Their point is again an apparently simple and clear one. In the early period, Justin Martyr, Irenaeus, Origen, Cyprian, Ambrose, and Augustine all claimed that the Word of God, the Scripture, was without error. Except for an occasional misprint, I have never found any of their references to the fathers to be misquoted or for that matter taken radically out of the immediate context of the chapter from which they quote. If this is such a frequent teaching of the formative period of Christianity, which is shared by all Christian communities, why does anyone oppose it? Because it is taken out of the wider context. Again to limit my examples, which I trust clarify the case, there is no doubt that Origen, the third-century Christian theologian born in Alexandria, was an inerrantist. He insisted that Scripture was perfect and true. Yet in interpreting Scripture he rather often looked at the literal meaning, found it to be improper in details, and then sought the truth in a deeper sense. After years of living in Caesarea of Palestine, he noticed that the description of certain places or the place names were incorrect, so he corrected them. His attention to literal detail was often thorough. And when the details seemed inappropriate or incorrect to him, he sought an allegorical meaning.

His allegory took other forms as well. In one of his most bizarre interpretations, Origen commented on the feeding of the five thousand. He insisted that Jesus would never say to people literally that they should sit on the grass as the biblical text says. The Son of God had too many important things to teach in too little time. Instead of the Lord commanding them to sit down so that they could be fed, Jesus obviously called them to put off the flesh, for, as the prophet Isaiah says, all flesh is grass.

In Origen's view Scriptural texts must be inerrant. But according to their literal meaning, they are often actually wrong in order to force us to the deeper, allegorical meaning. Origen never linked inerrancy and literal meaning as fundamentalist and evangelical supporters of inerrancy regularly do.

Augustine does rather similar things. For him the Bible is without error, but that errorlessness demands that a number of texts be interpreted allegorically rather than literally in order to keep the inerrancy intact. Augustine's works show that in his view when Scripture is read with simplistic literalness, it has errors of detail. Therefore it must be read allegorically to support its inerrancy. Such procedures from these ancient lights stand against an inerrantist's literal reading of Scripture. Inerrantists should not claim to teach an ancient doctrine when they strip that doctrine from its immediate corollaries and have the fathers defend inerrancy and literal interpretation, something they did not do.

The same kind of procedure is involved in Medieval and Reformation theologians. The latter are the more important for most Protestant inerrantists, since such Protestants are not certain that medieval Christianity understood Christian faith correctly. Luther supports the inerrancy of Scripture over against the occasionally mistaken opinions of the fathers. But he can also say when interpreting the numbers involved in Old Testament battles that there were probably 1,000 killed rather than the 80,000 the text says, because the numbers within the Old Testament are exaggerated. In his view what is meant is the whole people, not a specific number.[5] Calvin operates in a similar way. The point is that as a rule supporters of inerrancy within much of the history of the Church did not tie that doctrine to a literal reading of the texts.

There was, however, one period prior to the contemporary era in which important Christian teachers defended an inerrancy of biblical details read literally. Seventeenth-century Protestant divines interpreted the sixteenth-century Protestant creeds as meaning that every detail of the Bible was inspired and thus inerrant, even including the pointing of the Hebrew, that is, the later addition to the Hebrew consonants of vowels represented by a system of small signs. When scholarship discovered that the Massoretic texts and their pointing—the vowels—were far removed from the original texts, the position was abandoned. Divine inspiration, limited to the original writers, would not include those later pointers of the text. That was frightening to conservative Protestants since it made later interpreters inspired in some special way, a move that might be proposed as an analogue for the Roman arguments supporting the tradition or magisterium of the Church as the arbiter of Scriptural meaning.

In the midst of recent debates about the inerrancy of Scripture, a qualification of inspiration and the resultant inerrancy has occurred. Particularly in the nineteenth century when it became evident through the discovery of many older manuscripts that there were numerous textual problems in the manuscript tradition, inerrancy was restricted to the autographs, that is, the copies actually penned by the inspired writers or their scribes. This limitation of inerrancy to the autographs allowed for the difficulties in textual transmission without abandoning the inerrancy of the original, literal text. According to inerrantists what God inspired, in line with God's perfect nature, were the actual copies written by the chosen ones or their secretaries who took down what they dictated.

---

5. *Luther's Works,* ed. George Forrell (Philadelphia: Fortress Press, 1958) vol. 32, 11 notes his acceptance of inerrancy; *Luther's Works,* ed. Theodore Tappert (Philadelphia: Fortress Press, 1967) vol. 54, 452 indicates his sense of the wrong numbers. Donald Bloesch, *Essentials of Evangelical Theology, Vol. 1: God, Authority & Salvation* (San Francisco: Harper & Row, 1982) 65–66 cites both points.

Again the strangeness of this approach appears. First, it is a clear backing away from the inerrancy defended by seventeenth-century Protestant Orthodox divines, who first claimed that the texts in their hands were inerrant. To my knowledge few educated inerrantists, whether fundamentalist or evangelical, will claim that manuscripts or the critical texts of the Bible, as we now have them, are inerrant. Yet they are taking a weaker position on inerrancy than seventeenth-century Protestant Orthodoxy did. Of course, you may hear preachers who claim that the "authorized version" is the exact word of God. "If the King James Bible was good enough for Jesus, it's good enough for me." But sadly such claims are made by those who often do not know that the Bible was written in Hebrew, Aramaic, and Greek, and that the manuscripts we have do not all agree in every detail. They are unaware that it was a seventeenth-century English king who authorized the King James version, not God. While their ignorance may seem funny, it is sad when taken in the context of human concern. Snake-handlers, not far from where I live, illegally risk their lives by drinking poison and allowing themselves to be bitten by snakes on the basis of the longer ending of Mark used by the King James Version. That ending, however, is not in the oldest and best Greek manuscripts. And if you tell them that, they think you are a devil-inspired liberal who tampers with the Word of God. That is tragic.

Among the well-educated defenders of inerrancy, there is an odd compartmentalization in defense of this position. As in the arguments concerning the need to reformulate Scripture into logical propositions and the attacks on form critical study of inspired Scripture, the defense of inerrant autographs introduces error into God's plan, judgment, or character. If the inerrant statements of original Scripture are so important, essential to the argument for the truth of Christianity, why did God not see to it that the autographs were preserved? Wouldn't facing the contemporary situation be much simpler to withstand if we had perfect copies of the perfect pieces written by inspired authors? It is difficult not to caricature this position and thus do it an injustice. Yet this is the second time I have argued that defending inerrancy demands the introduction of error into God's efforts. God did not write Scripture in the proper syllogistic form; then God let the autographs slip away without seeing through his providence or seeing to it with his power that they were kept intact. I see these conclusions as unavoidable on the basis of the positions taken by inerrantists; I do not see those conclusions or the positions on which they are based as conservative. In my view God did inspire Scripture, using forms of persuasion that on occasion included rather tight logic. The destruction of the autographs is just life as usual. Originals wear out and cannot be circulated as widely as many copies. Life as usual does not break God or Scripture.

One final observation about supporters of inerrancy is in order. Among the most educated leadership a further development has taken place. While defending the doctrine and defining carefully what it entails, the seventeenth-century position has been abandoned on another front. As Carl Henry, a leading Evangelical insists that: "inerrancy does not imply that modern technological precision in reporting statistics and measurements, that conformity to modern historiographic method in reporting genealogies and other historical data, or that conformity to modern scientific method in reporting cosmological matters, can be expected from Biblical writers. . . . We have no right to impose upon the Biblical writers methods of classifying information that are specifically oriented to the scientific interests of our time, or to require their use of scientifically technical language, or to demand the computerized precision cherished by technological civilization." Henry goes on to insist that inerrancy "does not imply that verbal exactitude is required in New Testament quotation and use of Old Testament passages."[6]

The Chicago Statement on Biblical Inerrancy was issued by a conference held in October, 1978, attended by 284 Evangelicals and sponsored by the International Council on Biblical Inerrancy. Primarily an American group, these leaders confess that: "Being wholly and verbally God-given, Scripture is without error or fault in all its teaching, no less in what it states about God's acts in creation and the events of world history, and about its own literary origins under God, than in its witness to God's saving grace in individual lives. . . . The authority of Scripture is inescapably impaired if this total divine inerrancy is in any way limited

6. Carl F. H. Henry, *God, Revelation and Authority: Vol. IV, God Who Speaks and Shows* (Waco, Tex.: Word Books, 1979) 201–202.

or disregarded, or made relative to a view of truth contrary to the Bible's own."[7]

Within a later section of the document, they warn that history, poetry, hyperbole and metaphor must be taken literally as exactly what they are, since "nonchronological narration and imprecise citation were conventional and acceptable and violated no expectations in those days, we must not regard these things as faults when we find them in Bible writers. When total precision of a particular kind was not expected nor aimed at, it is no error not to have achieved it. Scripture is inerrant, not in the sense of being absolutely precise by modern standards, but in the sense of making good its claims and achieving the measure of focused truth at which its authors aimed." Oddities of grammar or spelling, descriptions of the phenomena in nature, false statements like those from the Devil or apparent discrepancies do not affect Scripture's inerrancy. This is not only death by a thousand qualifications, but also a kind of *semper eadem,* a view of "always the same" while obviously changing, that Evangelicals find so bizarre in Roman Catholic doctrine.[8] Yet there are a number of conservative Protestants, who reject the claim of inerrancy, who would support the view that Scripture is true "in the sense of making good its claims and achieving the measure of focused truth at which its authors aimed." I think that is descriptive of Scripture.

In perhaps the most stunning statement in the document, its writers and supporters insist that "it is not right to set the so-called phenomena of Scripture against the teaching of Scripture about itself."[9] I find this puzzling. What Scripture says in any of its parts cannot have an effect on what it teaches about its inspiration and thus on its inerrancy. Once the texts about biblical infallibility have been set in place, no amount of biblical data can be used to dislodge them.

7. "The Chicago Statement on Biblical Inerrancy," secs. 4 and 5 of the Short Statement, cited in Carl F. H. Henry, *God, Revelation and Authority, Vol. IV,* 212.

8. Tony Lane, "Evangelicalism and Roman Catholicism," *The Evangelical Quarterly* 51 (1989) 353 finds *semper eadem* to be the way Roman Catholicism regularly introduces change. He criticizes some "anti-Roman protestants" for accepting this "counter-reformation catholic myth."

9. Carl F. H. Henry, *God, Revelation and Authority, Vol. IV,* 211–219, specifically 212, "A Short Statement" 4. and 5., and "Exposition: Infallibility, Inerrancy, Interpretation," 217–218.

That claim raises two points. First, it is correct for these people to deny that they are taking over the seventeenth-century sense of inerrancy.[10] The seventeenth-century doctrine was much stronger and tighter than this one as I have indicated. Second, if inerrancy is not affected by the words of Scripture, why is it important to use inerrancy as a description of Scripture? It can be fairly asked whether or not a definition or description holds if it does not fit the data. If the Bible is not perfect in its details because the eras in which it was written did not always have interests in such perfection, then it follows that interpretations, which insist that the Bible claims "perfection," are themselves imperfect. It is very odd indeed to import definitions of inerrancy into the interpretation of biblical texts like John 10, 2 Peter 1, and 2 Timothy 3 when the actual reading of the content of Scripture does not support those interpretations.

Perhaps Fundamentalists and Evangelicals who support inerrancy would be better advised to abandon the term "inerrant" for Scripture if it is not specifically employed by the Bible when it makes claims about its own character, if it depends on a crumbled philosophical foundationalism, if it has not served well in the history of the Church for keeping commentators to a more literal interpretation of Scripture, and if it constantly raises the specter of a test that cannot be passed by the biblical texts. Clark Pinnock, a noted Evangelical who formerly defended inerrancy, has argued first in articles that a moratorium on the use of the word was in order, and now in his book *The Scripture Principle* has suggested that it should be used but with a much more honest and thus less tight definition.[11] A number of well-informed Evangelicals have gone further and argued the case for the Bible's trustworthiness, its character as the Word of God, without the use of the term "inerrancy."[12] It is difficult to see what the positive function of the term or concept could be. The term "trustwor-

10. Ibid., "Article XVI," 214.

11. Clark Pinnock, *The Scripture Principle* (San Francisco: Harper & Row, 1984).

12. Carl F. H. Henry, *God, Revelation and Authority, Vol. IV*, 162–195 names Dewey Beegle, Donald Bloesch, G. C. Berkouwer, David Hubbard, Jack Rodgers, and other Evangelicals who do not hold to what he considers to be the strictest interpretation of inerrancy.

thy," or something similar covers the deep Christian sense that God has not left us alone without a clear word. The negative function of inerrancy too often has been to seal off the Bible from historical-critical investigation. At least since the Reformation and particularly since the seventeenth century it has apparently provided Protestantism with an infallible guide over against the Roman Catholic sense of infallible guidance from tradition: from councils, from the Doctors of the Church, from the magisterium, and *ex cathedra* from the papacy. But biblical inerrancy can no longer serve to insulate a Protestant from tradition as if there were no important Christian Tradition to which the Bible reader, interpreter, or preacher belongs.

One very positive advancement among Evangelicals in recent decades is the discussion of Tradition and tradition. Some of them are beginning to move beyond the *sola scriptura,* the Scripture alone, principle that has dominated Protestant conservatives since the Reformation. Most Protestants would have been willing to follow William Chillingworth's slogan: "The Bible, I say, the Bible only, is the religion of Protestants."[13] Some contemporary Evangelicals still accept that view.[14] Other Evangelicals, however, have taken positions that honor Christians who lived out the faith in their own age. David Wells and A.N.S. Lane, both noted Evangelicals, have written about a new awakening to the necessity of recognizing the oneness of a common Christian Tradition with a capital "T," while putting the smaller "t" traditions under its judgment. Wells looks to a further study of the patristic period as one of shared tradition.[15] Lane distinguishes between three senses of the relationship between Scripture and tradition: an early patristic view in which they coincide as in Irenaeus, Tertullian, and Vincent of Lérins' famous statement of universality, antiq-

13. A.N.S. Lane, "Scripture, Tradition and Church: An Historical Survey," *Vox Evangelica* 9 (1975) 39–44.

14. By no means have all Evangelicals moved beyond *sola scriptura.* See the statement of the Theological Commission of the World Evangelical Fellowship in "An Evangelical Perspective on Roman Catholicism," *Evangelical Review of Theology* 10 (1986) 343. Reprinted in *Roman Catholicism: A Contemporary Evangelical Perspective,* ed. Paul G. Schrotenboer (Grand Rapids, Mich.: Baker Book House, 1987) 16.

15. David Wells, "Tradition: A Meeting Place for Catholic and Evangelical Theology?," *Christian Scholars Review* 5 (1975) 50–61.

uity, and consensus; a patristic view further developed in later periods that saw tradition as supplementary or a second source of revelation; and the Reformation view that tradition is ancillary, a tool to assist in understanding Scripture. Lane plumps for the latter because of his deep sense of Scriptural perspicuity and sufficiency, its clarity and wholeness. Yet at the same time he recognizes that it is impossible for each age to avoid doctrinal development in favor of a simple summary of biblical teaching.[16] If you are old enough to remember the early parodies from Andy Griffith, you can see the importance of this change. Fewer and fewer evangelical preachers will settle the issue with a raised King James, leather-covered, embossed-with-your-name-in-gold, copy of the Bible by saying: "Why do I believe that? Because it's in the Book!"

On the Roman Catholic side lies a growing appreciation of Scripture. There is good reason for that. From the patristic period on, the Bible played an important role within both Western and Eastern Catholicism. In truth Roman Catholicism has always been interested in Scripture. Certainly significant Roman Catholic energy has been spent on other enterprises. Yet one of the reasons we do not know as much about biblical exegesis within Roman Catholicism as we might has been both the lack of frequently copied commentaries and the lack of interest in creating critical texts and translations of those commentaries we have in manuscript form. Most medieval and some patristic biblical commentaries languish in European libraries without champions to bring them to our attention. It has been of more interest to most students, particularly of the medieval period, to look at the philosophical and cultural aspects of the institutions and people of import. Those who have the competence to read the manuscripts often confess that the contents of the commentaries are dry, not particularly new or exciting. But the existence of those commentaries in various forms lets us know that patristic and medieval figures themselves did not find the Bible dry or uninteresting. Until we have a clearer view of what forces brought those commentaries into existence and what influence they had, we must be careful not to leave interest in Scripture only at the manuscript-

16. A.N.S. Lane, "Scripture, Tradition and Church: An Historical Survey," 37–55.

copying level. Many evangelical Protestants have offered praise—
sometimes begrudgingly—to those who kept and copied biblical
manuscripts. But few conservative Protestants know and thus have
accounted for the remarkable interest in the Bible during these
earlier periods.

Even the stalwart hero of present Roman Catholic conservatism,
Thomas Aquinas, had great respect for Scripture. It is ironic to
think of this flaming liberal from the thirteenth century as the
bastion of conservatism in the present. He wrote commentaries
not only on the *Sentences* of Peter Lombard, but Scripture itself. One of my prized possessions is the nineteenth-century English translation of Aquinas' commentary on the gospels, a
compilation of patristic and early medieval interpretations in
which Aquinas himself says little or nothing, only arranging the
previous commentary tradition. I seldom preach from the gospels
without looking to those volumes. In fact I have used them so
much that they needed to be sent to the bindery while I was away
from my usual teaching assignments doing these lectures at John
Carroll University.

Precisely within his *Summa Theologica,* the great systematic
theology he produced, Aquinas indicates that Scripture alone
teaches what is primary; all else is secondary. He certainly was
interested in theology, in what the tradition before him had said
and how he could use Aristotle to organize a presentation of the
faith for his contemporary world. We must never forget that he
was a missionary theologian, one concerned not with writing a
bizarre new theology and thus getting tenure somewhere, but with
catching up to Islam which had a better grasp of Aristotle than
did most Westerners. His first run on the systematic was a mission manual, the *Summa Contra Gentiles,* for those of his order
in Spain, on how to meet the challenge of Islam and Judaism.
Within the later *Summa Theologica* he ordered things almost alge-
braically. But if you can remember algebraic formulae, anything
outside the parenthesis controls all that goes on within that
parenthesis. If I understand him correctly, Thomas viewed Scripture as outside the parenthesis controlling all that was within.

In recent years some brilliant Roman Catholic scholars have
insisted that the Council of Trent did not teach two sources of
revelation when it met to describe Catholic teaching during the

struggles of the sixteenth century. The Latin *et,* the little word "and" which links Scripture and tradition in Trent's official pronouncements, seems to have been a compromise. Some insisted that tradition could make plain what Scripture had said and add what it had not said. The Spanish interpreters of Trent in the seventeenth century, much as the Protestant Orthodoxy of that century, hardened the position. For those interpreters the Council of Trent demanded that God had given two sources of revelation, Scripture, and tradition. But the *Görres Gesellschaft* of Germany and Roman Catholic scholars like Josef Geiselmann and Georges Tavard, went through the letters and diaries of the council and found that most of the participants demanded the language of "Scripture and Tradition" in order to avoid a sense of two sources of revelation.[17] If true—and that interpretation has been contested particularly by Lennerz[18]—it is utterly remarkable. Roman Catholic moderates at Trent did not let the pressure of the Reformation shambles harden their positions, but reaffirmed an understanding that had long been a part of their own heritage.

Whether or not that historical description proves to be the most accurate as it is restudied by contemporary historians, one fact is secure. At Vatican II the participants rejected curial language about two sources of revelation and returned to language of Scripture and Tradition. That means that any Roman Catholic may again look to Scripture as normative and not speak of tradition as a second source of revelation, although tradition is not seen as antithetical to Scripture, and the magisterium, the living teaching office, is viewed as the authority for the interpretation of Scripture.[19]

Since the Papal document *Divino afflante Spiritu* in 1943, Roman Catholic Biblical scholarship has reasserted its tremen-

17. Josef Geiselmann, *Die Heilige Schrift und die Tradition. Zu den neueren Kontroversen über das Verhältnis der Heiligen Schrift zu den nichtgeschriebenen Traditionen* (Freiburg: Herder, 1962). Geiselmann, *The Meaning of Tradition,* trans. W. J. O'Hara (New York: Herder and Herder, 1966) contains the first three chapters of the larger work. Georges Tavard, *Holy Writ or Holy Church: The Crisis of the Protestant Reformation* (Westport, Conn.: Greenwood Press, 1978).

18. H. Lennerz, "Scriptura sola?," *Gregorianum* 40 (1959) 38-53.

19. *Vatican Council II: Conciliar and Post Conciliar Documents,* ed. Austin Flannery, O.P., New Rev. Ed. (Northport, N.Y.: Costello Publishing Company, 1984) 58. *Dei verbum* 11-26, 758-765.

dous influence.[20] As a professor in what some view as a conservative Protestant seminary, I can tell you that nearly every biblical book which we study requires us to read a Roman Catholic commentary. In many ways Roman Catholic scholarship has understood the place of the Bible in the community of faith more clearly than has much of the so-called Protestant establishment of scriptural study. I know numerous Protestant Scripture specialists who have great difficulty seeing the Bible as the book of worshipping people. The study of Scripture within the contemporary Church owes much to the insight and balance of Roman Catholic scholarship.

Cardinal Ratzinger looks with a careful eye and powerful head at doctrinal developments throughout the papal domain and thus is often no party guest for Catholic or Protestant. Having taught in Tübingen during the period when Hans Küng was under investigation, I know Cardinal Ratzinger often was not viewed as a welcome friend. Yet he emphasized in his 1988 Erasmus lecture, that it is important for biblical interpreters to employ the historical-critical methods with a growing sense of treating those methods historically and critically.[21] That is an interest which many Protestant Evangelicals share. Unlike Fundamentalists who have often called for the demise of historical criticism or prematurely celebrated its death, many Evangelicals have incorporated careful, critical study of Scripture into their regular practice. But at the same time those Evangelicals have offered comments on what they find to be the presuppositions of some scholarly study of the Bible. Particularly in a world that scientifically has come to grasp the force of Heisenberg's principle concerning the perpetual subjectivity of the observer, and Kuhn's insistence that science operates not without presuppositions but within a controlling paradigm that suggests topics of investigations, defines the methods used, and then eventually dies, it is appropriate to

20. "Divino afflante Spiritu," encyclical letter of Pope Pius XII, September 30, 1943, in *Bible Interpretation,* ed. James J. Megivern (Wilmington, N.C.: McGrath Publishing, 1978) 316–342.

21. Joseph Ratzinger, "Biblical Interpretation in Crisis: On the Question of the Foundations and Approaches of Exegesis Today," *Biblical Interpretation in Crisis: The Ratzinger Conference on Bible and Church,* ed. Richard John Neuhaus (Grand Rapids, Mich: William B. Eerdmans, 1989) 1–23.

examine critically the historical-critical study of Scripture. That task neither demands nor supports the entrenched opposition of Fundamentalism. Instead it involves an open discussion of what historical study entails.

On those bases evangelical Protestants and Roman Catholics have much to discuss. Within their communities, many are willing to investigate the place of Scripture and Tradition. Richard McBrien notes in his tome *Catholicism* that Lutherans and Roman Catholics agreed in 1978 that the Bible is normative for all the Church's proclamation and teaching.[22] From 1977–1984 an Evangelical-Roman Catholic Dialogue on Mission met four times. The discussions were difficult; no great plan of union came from the efforts. Yet their joint statement published in 1986 shows that it is possible for the two groups to find a limited yet common witness, one in which the evangelical Protestants honor the heritage of Christian faith outside the Bible and Roman Catholics honor the Bible.[23] But such interest in the Bible within Roman Catholicism is not limited to biblical scholars and representatives in ecumenical discussions. I recently taught a course on the Trinity at the Abbey of New Clairvaux in Vina, California. One of the Trappists in the class always brought what some of his fellow monks called his "coloring book." It was a worn Jerusalem Bible, cover torn, that has been read over the years with different magic markers in hand. He and his colleagues could not only refer to the fathers and the giants of Cistercian spirituality, but also the Scripture itself. While teaching at New Clairvaux I met both or-

22. Richard McBrien, *Catholicism,* Study Edition (San Francisco: Harper & Row, 1981) 839. That agreement also included a sense that "the Church expresses its faith and fulfills its mission especially in the ministry of word and sacrament, supervised and coordinated by specific ministries and structures, including the ministry of bishops and the bishop of Rome."

23. Basil Meeking and John Stott, eds., *The Evangelical-Roman Catholic Dialogue on Mission, 1977–1984: A Report* (Grand Rapids, Mich.: William B. Eerdmans, 1986) show that tough discussions took place with interesting recognitions of the weaknesses on both sides. Other efforts, however, like the *Thailand Report: Witness to Nominal Christians Among Roman Catholics* (Wheaton: Lausanne Occasional Paper, no. 10, 1980) and "An Evangelical Perspective on Roman Catholicism," *Evangelical Review of Theology* 10 (1986) 342–364 and 11 (1987) 78–94, reprinted as *Roman Catholicism: A Contemporary Evangelical Perspective,* ed. Paul G. Schrotenboer (Grand Rapids, Mich: Baker Book House, 1987), indicate a continued distrust of Roman Catholicism.

dained priests and people involved in the Rite of Christian Initiation programs that prepare adults for baptism and membership in Roman Catholic churches. They also indicated the instruction includes much Scripture. Such experiences from within Roman Catholic communities of many descriptions are anything but rare.

As we turn to the task set before us by the rest of this volume, we shall be involved in the process of looking at Scripture and Tradition. Our first question must be, can the Nicene-Constantinopolitan Creed, the most ecumenically accepted creed of the early Church, provide a tradition that will assist us in understanding the biblical and traditional teachings concerning God, Christ, the Holy Spirit, and the Church as well as worship and life?

# Part II
# catholic Christian Faith

# 3

# The Nicene-Constantinopolitan Creed

The Nicene-Constantinopolitan Creed is said to be the most widely held and frequently confessed of all the early Christian creeds. In its recent studies of "The Apostolic Faith" the World Council of Churches has turned to this creed as expressive of the shared heritage of ecumenical or catholic Christianity. Part of that decision doubtless rested upon the 1600 year anniversary of the 381 Council of Constantinople, but there were other grounds. This creed, an early and eventually an ecumenical one, contains many of the central convictions held by most if not all Christians. It does not meet the qualifications of what has been believed by everyone in every place during every age, the inspiring ideal which Vincent of Lérins proclaimed in fifth-century France. But even Vincent knew that such an ideal was not as often achieved as he wished. This creed does represent a rather broad consensus of what many Christians in many regions throughout the centuries have accepted as fundamental to Christian faith. Both leading Protestants and Catholics have acknowledged it as a meeting place even though they may approach it from various vantage points.[1]

1. The Lutheran Edmund Schlink, "Die biblische Grundlage des Glaubens-bekentnisses des 2. ökumenischen Konzils 381," *La signification et l'actualité du IIe concile oecuménique pour le monde chrétien d'aujourd'hui,* Les études théologiques de chambesy 2 (Chambesy: Éditions du centre orthodoxe du patriarcat oecuménique, 1982) 139 accepts such a claim. The evangelical Protestant John Jefferson Davis, *Foundations of Evangelical Theology* (Grand Rapids, Mich.: Baker Book House, 1984) 221–243 refers to the four ecumenical creeds: the Apostles', this Nicene, the Chalcedonian, and the Athanasian. The Roman Catholic

This so-called Nicene Creed often appears in mainline Protestant, Catholic, Anglican, and Orthodox liturgies and thus provides a reference point which goes beyond conservative Protestant and Roman Catholic circles toward a description of catholic Christian Faith. Because it is often confessed during worship, it provides a rather remarkable shared position.

The Nicene-Constantinopolitan Creed is Trinitarian; it deals with God the Father, Christ the Son and the Holy Spirit, the life-giver, in three articles. A letter from a council of Constantinople in 382, a year after the ecumenical council, employs the language of three persons in one nature, three *hypostases* in one *ousia,* and claims that those terms were a part of the discussion at the 381 council. Although not invoked in the creed itself, such language provided a background understanding which forms part of the context of the creed. Within the creed, at least one heavily laden philosophical term, *homoousios,* "of the same essence," was used to clarify the doctrine of the Trinity.

We must, however, notice two things. First, this creed intended to return to the more biblical statements which undergird a sense of Trinity at the same time that it kept the term *homoousios* which does not appear in Scripture and has deep philosophical roots. Once again the faithful tried to stay within the confines of Scripture. The so-called "orthodox" had been stung in their debate with the Arians when they were constantly accused of dragging in non-biblical phrases. This creed has the smell and taste of Scripture at the same time that it does not hesitate to restate certain

---

Berard L. Marthaler, *The Creed* (Mystic, Conn.: Twenty-Third Publications, 1987) vii notes that Paul VI's "Credo of the People of God," printed in 1968, was an attempt to rephrase the Nicene-Constantinopolitan Creed for modernity. Marthaler himself treats both the Apostles' and the 381 creed in his book.

On p. 20 he selects my tradition as one that rejects the use of creeds through its aphorism: no creed but Christ. The point of the aphorism is the rejection of creeds as dogmatic formulations which must be accepted word for word in order to be a Christian, as official statements of what the faith must be. That need not deny the use of creeds as historical guides for the study of the faith, indeed as important helps for understanding the continuity of the faith. The best theologian in my tradition, William Robinson, *Essays on Christian Unity* (London: James Clark, 1924) 63–98 argued for the importance of this creed. People within our congregations often discover it as a good summary of what they learn from the Bible.

positions in non-scriptural words. Those who wrote it and those who signed it hoped to make clear what they thought the intent of the Bible was. The Church leaders at the councils of Nicaea and Constantinople used a word like *homoousios* in order to say what they found in Scripture, to contextualize the faith for their era. They could assemble a number of biblical passages which claimed the Son and the Spirit were divine; anyone at any time can do the same.

Second, this Nicene-Constantinopolitan Creed presents historical problems when it is used as a basis for ecumenical discussion. In fact, it almost fits the repeated category of the bizarre I have employed throughout the previous chapters. Christians usually call it the Nicene Creed when it is confessed within church liturgies. In a certain sense, however, that title is incorrect because the Council of Nicaea in 325 adopted a somewhat different creed, one which has no long paragraph on the Holy Spirit, and does have some different sentences about God and Christ. In the technical literature scholars call it the Nicene-Constantinopolitan Creed, because the Council of Constantinople in 381 appears to have adopted it. But the proceedings of that Council in Constantinople have been lost, so we have no record of what happened. The Council of Chalcedon in 451 referred to this creed as coming from the Council of Constantinople in 381, but certain bishops attending the Chalcedon assembly seemed to be surprised by this document, almost as if they had not seen it before. For that reason some scholars have claimed that it was never mentioned before 451 and that it could not have come from the Constantinopolitan Council of 381.[2] Thus we might have a creed called "Nicene" which doesn't come from Nicaea and perhaps should not be called "Nicene-Constantinopolitan" because it might not come from Constantinople. Yet it is still the most ecumenically accepted Christian creed even if we did not know with absolute certainty what its name is, what group first proposed it, or what council first adopted it. Odd.

Near the beginning of the twentieth century and for about fifty years thereafter majority scholarly opinion considered this creed to be a baptismal creed from Jerusalem which preceded the 381

2. J.N.D. Kelly, *Early Christian Creeds,* 3rd ed. (London: Longmans, 1972) chs. 7 and 10.

Constantinopolitan council. The best evidence for that was a group of lectures given by a Jerusalem bishop named Cyril in the 360s and the appearance of this creed in a work from 374 by Epiphanius, a fiery old heresy hunter from Crete. The lectures of the Jerusalem bishop, however, do not treat this creed fully; they have only chapter headings which specifically recall most of it. The text of Epiphanius' work has come to us in poor condition. It is probable that some later scribe corrected the creed used in the piece so that Epiphanius would look more orthodox. As you can see this tale becomes more bizarre by the minute.

Now enter the creedal studies of the last few decades. A number of specialists have made some corrections which create a picture not only less unusual, but in fact, rather remarkable at three points. First, the loss of the proceedings of this Constantinopolitan Council of 381 may have been influenced partially by the lack of the broadest kind of representation. No representatives from the Western sections of the empire attended. Indeed, Rome did not accept this 381 council for some time apparently because the council insisted that the see of Constantinople was second only to Rome in power and rank. Some bishops in Rome during the fifth and sixth centuries were not certain that any religious center was "second" to Rome. They saw their theological heritage as so outstanding and the political power of Constantinople as so threatening that second place was not to be conceded to Constantinople's bishop. Unlike the interminable American arguments about who is number one, this debate concerned who was number two. The way to make sense of it is to question whether political power was the ultimate basis of the argument. Since the emperor had his permanent residence at Constantinople, the Constantinopolitan bishop would have had a great advantage. His mouth rather than the Roman bishop's would be closer to the imperial ear. Thus Rome joined with Alexandria, which was offended because it was sure that it occupied second place, and made life miserable for Constantinople. Rome argued that the council of 381 at Constantinople was not ecumenical, but provincial, yet the real issue was the fear of losing influence.

This attempt by Rome to stifle the authority of the Constantinopolitan council is instructive. Rome has had a remarkable history of being a bastion of orthodoxy in early Christianity. But on this question, for decades it suffered from defensiveness. Rome, however, had both the courage and the insight eventually to accept an Eastern council as ecumenical even though it did not send delegates and did not control the decision. Rome's influence was felt in the person of Theodosius, the emperor, who had decreed in 380 that all Christian churches should confess a Trinitarian faith, one similar to that confessed by Damasus, the bishop of Rome. Theodosius called the council. But this indirect Roman influence, even backed by imperial might, did not originally satisfy the Roman see. The important issue, however, is still that Rome finally accepted the 381 Council of Constantinople as ecumenical, and thus put its error behind it. The greatest of the Western sees came out in favor of an Eastern creed. Truth could appear in places which Rome did not personally oversee and directly influence. Such insight must never be lost.

Second, recent research has found writings in which something like this creed appears. Thus it was not unknown for seventy years before the Council of Chalcedon in 451; it was just primarily unknown to a number of Western Roman bishops, or supporters of Rome against Constantinople. On that basis it seems much more likely that the creed itself was framed at the council of 381 even if it did have some precursor from elsewhere. If that is true it deserves its name Nicene-Constantinopolitan.

Third, the newer scholarship has shown us that the creed of Constantinople was referred to as Nicene because these fourth- and fifth-century Church leaders did not think of Christian faith as inerrantly or literally fixed in a particular formula. When the Church historians of the era said that the Council of Constantinople confirmed the Nicene creed, they probably meant that the 381 council developed this creed which is so clearly similar to but not the same as the creed from the 325 Council of Nicaea. Indeed a creed from the Council of Constantinople would be called Nicene after the 325 council because it had the same kind of content, because it had the same flavor.

This understanding of "Nicene" involves a significant insight. Early Christians could recognize acceptable content in formulae which were not exactly the same. We moderns need to recognize Christian content in the sentences of people who do not say things exactly as we do. We need to find ways to identify similar speech.

Christian faith comes from people, not parrots. The whole purpose of the lectures which I gave and these chapters as written is to invite a predominately Roman Catholic audience to consider that conservative Protestants are saying many of the same things with somewhat different language. That is a solid principle built into the ecumenical councils of the patristic period, the one era of Christian history beyond that of the New Testament which all Christians fully share. Would that we all had the courage and the trust to attempt such expressions of faith with an eye to the center of our history and the needs of the present age.

My own recognition of these significant similarities appeared first within deeply-felt experiences at Yale University and has continued through contacts with Roman Catholics within my academic speciality, the field of patristic studies. After growing up in the Midwest and attending college and seminary in Tennessee and Oklahoma, I arrived with my wife, Carol, and baby daughter, Lisa, at New Haven, Connecticut, in 1967. Although I always gravitated to foreign students during previous educational experiences, I had never attended a world-class, internationally oriented university. Many of my views and habits were raw. One of the shocking events of the first months was to go to a party of fellow graduate students in which hymns that formed a part of my heart-felt worship tradition were sung by a male quartet as humorous entertainment. Although I had not left the United States, I was indeed an innocent abroad.

With the exception of a few friends I soon discovered that many of my colleagues in the department were what conservative Protestants call "liberals." To my jangled nerves an imposing number of them seemed interested primarily in good jobs in university departments of religious studies in which what I considered to be commitment to Christian faith was burdensome, perhaps even a hindrance, to the academic study of things Christian. Then I met a number of Roman Catholics. In each case and among various temperaments and orders, I found women and men, some who had Church vocations and some who did not, people who came to Yale to acquire one of the best educations possible in order to serve the Church. Some of them strained against a traditionalism they found restraining. But in nearly every instance I was able to resonate with their sense of the faith. I did not see or say things exactly as they did, but the situation enabled me to recognize that we held common goals.[3]

That impression has been strengthened through my contacts with Roman Catholics in the field of patristic studies. There have been "liberal" and "conservative" variations, "ordained" and "lay" professors and students, but nearly always some deep sense of the importance of tradition and revelation, and enough shared vocabulary and interest to talk about significant things in common ways. I have felt the resonance and have been moved by it. Some of them have called me to account for my apparent discomfort with aspects of my Anabaptist Protestant heritage as I have helped them recover some of the strengths of Roman tradition as they made their way into new or renewed forms of Christian living. It has been and is no difficulty for me to expect Christian faith and virtue among the Roman Catholic people I meet.

The history of the acceptance of the ecumenical status of the Nicene-Constantinopolitan Creed and of the council that proclaimed it might have alerted me to expect that kind of experience among my Roman Catholic colleagues at Yale, but in the first year I did not know that much about those particular events of history. Now that I have spent some time in their study, however, they do not present only positive features. At the same time that we praise the strengths of the Nicene-Constantinopolitan Creed, we also must recognize the weaknesses of this most ecumenical statement of faith.

Unlike those attending the Robber Synod of Ephesus in 449, the participants in the 381 council and their supporters did not beat anyone to death. They did, however, practice their own brand of ecclesiastical politics. Gregory Nazianzen, orthodox bishop of Constantinople, became the president of the 381 council when the first president died. But certain representatives from Egyptian churches, particularly those from Alexandria, pressed a case against Nazianzen's being bishop of Constantinople, let alone president of the council. They insisted that, in defiance of canon law, Gregory had come to Constantinople after being the bishop at two sites in Cappadocia, his home city of Nazianzus and an-

---

3. Although it is not the point of this book I had the same kind of experiences with Orthodox friends.

other small town named Sasima. Although their crossed t's and dotted i's may have been correct, their motivation was again to weaken the see of Constantinople so that only Alexandria could be seen as second to Rome. Gregory was not a particularly patient fellow and eventually resigned with both a stunning final speech rebuking such political moves and later comments about the problems of councils. He referred to his colleagues at the council in various writings as cawing crows or as a gaggle of geese and warned a young cousin that such assemblies threatened one's faith, even one's soul. It is not merely sixteenth-century Protestants who questioned the infallibility of councils. Rome questioned the validity of the Second Ecumenical Council for a number of decades and Gregory Nazianzen, a former president of the council and one of the three hierarchs of Eastern Orthodoxy, also found it wanting.

More detrimentally, this council was called, supported and in some ways dominated by the emperor Theodosius. He had already made it imperial legal policy that the Trinitarian faith held by Damasus of Rome would be the faith of the realm. Perhaps we are wise enough in the present era to see the horror of that; perhaps not. We often shudder at the *Deutsche Christen* who backed Hitler's policies but are thrilled when American civil religion throws us a crumb. How nostalgic some of us can be for the opening prayers at football games. We forget that Constantinian establishment is often a curse, not a blessing, whatever clothes it now wears (if any).

A Christian as the head of the empire thrilled Eusebius of Caesarea when Constantine made Christianity legal and then favored. Had any of us lived under emperors who mounted persecutions against the Church, a believing emperor would have seemed to be a gift of God. Yet Eusebius made a damning mistake; he decided that the emperor should be the bishop for those outside the Church. In line with Eusebius' views from seventy years earlier, Theodosius only wanted to get on with the political process so that peace would come to the empire. The religious pillar had to hold part of the weight of societal need. If the Nicene-Constantinopolitan Creed has become the most ecumenical because it justifies the melding of Church and state, because it indicates that earthly political rulers will determine the nature of

Christian faith, then it should be given back to the earthly and buried. If it is to be accepted on any level because it comes from an alliance between the state and the Church, then it must be rejected. Caesar is not God.

The singular test of this creed must be whether or not it legitimately represents Christian faith. In the midst of answering such questions, the Bible in the Church is the touchstone. Even the use of the *homoousios* is not the proof that tradition must be more than Scripture.[4] Athanasius of Alexandria, who fought for orthodoxy at the 325 council, used the word *homoousios* in his defense of the faith against the Arians much less than we might suppose. Quotations from the Gospel of John are more frequent. If we look at the work of the second president of the 381 council, Gregory Nazianzen, we find his debates with his opponents rooted in the Bible. Within his *Theological Orations* Gregory uses over seven hundred fifty scriptural citations and allusions to establish his points. What he argues is that the Trinitarian positions he holds make better sense of more Scripture than the subordinating positions given to the Son and the Spirit which his opponents hold. The *homoousios* for Nazianzen is not a Hellenistic concept and term that is added to Scripture, but the truth of the Bible contextualized for his time. A large portion of the Nicene-Constantinopolitan Creed is Scripture restated; the rest is Scripture contextualized.

Such insight does not mean, however, that the reception of the council and its creed as ecumenical is insignificant.[5] If the creed of a council is accepted as catholic, as universal, on bases that reaffirm the place of culture or political power over the Lordship of Christ, such acceptance will eventually be seen as false, or the Church will suffer. If tradition insists upon positions that falsify the claims we have in Scripture, it must be brought to account. Aelred Squire, a Carthusian monk, has caught the point:

---

4. John Courtney Murray, *The Problem of God: Yesterday and Today,* "The St. Thomas More Lectures, 1" (New Haven: Yale University Press, 1964) ch. 2, makes that case quite well, but does not understand that *homoousios* is a contextualization of the faith during the fourth century within Hellenistic culture, not the backbone of any Christian community.

5. André Halleaux, "La réception du symbole oecuménique de Nicée à Chalcédoine," *Éphémérides théologicae Lovanienses* 61 (1985) 5–47.

creeds help us "keep intact in our minds the frontiers of the mysteries to whose living reality we must constantly return." They have never been viewed as a "substitute for that picture of the total mystery of salvation which the Scriptures more obscurely and more diversely embody"; indeed the place of Scripture "in the Church's liturgy and the teaching of her great masters has never been supplanted or fundamentally challenged."[6] As noted earlier, the growth of Scripture studies and their influence in theological reflection within Roman Catholicism bodes well for the future, because they are biblical, catholic and Roman. Protestants have "traditions of men" which must be called to account and Roman Catholics can help do that. Both Catholics and Protestants must look for the catholic Tradition which has assisted the Church in being faithful within every generation.

The Nicene-Constantinopolitan Creed has other severe limitations of content as do all the creeds. Although it is primarily a Christological creed in terms of quantity, it still mentions nothing of Jesus' teaching other than perhaps connotations of his claim to Messiahship. It deals with nothing about his life among people other than his birth, crucifixion, death, burial, and resurrection. Those elements are extremely important, but not enough. Much of the debate about who Jesus is must refer to more of his teaching and life than the Nicene-Constantinopolitan Creed provides. That is not primarily a position taken by a Protestant who puts Scripture above the traditions of men, but the view of scholars who have reflected upon the creed. I first had such a stunning deficiency pointed out to me by a professor in a Roman Catholic faculty of theology.[7] The creed helps us organize and state in short paragraphs what we find to be significant about Christian faith, but it does not replace the gospels or the epistles. It is creed and New Testament, Tradition and Scripture, which make us whole.

What treasure we have in this statement of faith is one in earthen vessels. To turn one of Gregory Nazianzen's metaphors, even a

6. Aelred Squire, *Asking the Fathers: The Art of Meditation and Prayer* (New York: Paulist Press, 1973) 118.

7. See Hermann Josef Vogt, "Exegese und Kirchengeschichte," *Theologische Quartalschrift* 159 (1979) 45, a professor in the Roman Catholic Faculty at the University of Tübingen, Germany, who notes that all the ancient creeds give no information about Jesus' life and teachings, and thus are always deficient.

gaggle of geese can on occasion produce something other than a goose egg. It is never clear that any particular council will express the consensus of the faithful; but even one that has large flaws may also have great strengths. The context of a council called by the dominant political figure in order to ratify his assessment of the faith can only yield Christian results through the imposition of another design. The ecclesiastical power plays by some of the council's members were abominable, but the insight into Christian faith represented by the creed was abundant.

Yet, like nearly all the better-known creeds of ancient Christianity, this one has a negative, exclusive side. It is not as scathing as the Western Athanasian Creed which many Churches have let slide out of the public eye. The anathemas, the curses, of that creed almost make your hair stand on end. This creed is still more oriented toward a public confession than is the Chalcedonian Creed which has the form of a statement of doctrine; this creed says "we believe in" rather than "It should be believed." Each of us as a Christian must confess that our positive statements will have negative undertones that give us grief. At the same time we must understand that there are representations of Christianity which are not faithful but heretical. It will never do to suggest that any definition of Christian faith will do. We must see some aspects of negative statements as much as a sign of our own nagging sinfulness as they are signs of the waywardness of brothers and sisters in Christ. Creeds have too often been employed as ultimate tests of fellowship which have divided the body of Christ unnecessarily.

In my own specific Church tradition, which goes back to Scottish Reformed Churches, there was a time in the late eighteenth century in which no person could partake of the Eucharist, the Lord's Supper, unless that person could satisfactorily explain the meaning of the accepted Westminster Creed. Metal tokens were given by the presbytery to the people who had passed the test. Only those with the tokens could receive the bread and wine. No token; no Eucharist. Simple trust in Jesus would not do. Reliance upon the biblical narratives retold within the Tradition of the Church was not enough. Making Christian faith into required systematic theology can never be appropriate for it demands that only the most mentally gifted can fully give their allegiance to the Lord. Roman Catholics have usually known better than that; many conservative Protestants have also seen its weakness, for such procedures are now rare.

One final note about the council is appropriate. The creed contains no detailed ethical commands in its few lines. We might suggest that the small format of a creed does not provide space for any such attention to how we should live the Christian life. Indeed both the Council of Nicaea in 325 and the Council of Constantinople in 381 set out a number of so-called "canons," ecclesiastical laws, which were meant to deal with specific problems found particularly among the leaders of the Church, but ones which involved all members within the congregations. The councils evidently were following a pattern that had been in existence for at least a hundred years if not longer. The Church had attempted to devise its own sense of law so that believers would know what things to avoid and how to react in situations where virtues were stained, relationships were strained and conduct was questionable.

This decision and its ratification in these ecumenical councils points up three things. First, doctrine and ethics were being separated into distinct forms with the result that creed and canon might lose their sense of interconnection. Doctrinal heretics were often accused of immoral conduct, but the moral conduct of faithful leaders could be examined without questioning their sense of doctrine. This fatal separation finds similarities in modern attempts to devise specialized places where specific issues will be discussed. Doctrine is one thing, ethics another. Thus those who would suggest that creed sets ethics, that the narratives which stand behind this creed have within them calls to discipleship which cannot be separated from the stories, are often misunderstood or looked at with blank stares. Whether among Protestant Evangelicals or among Roman Catholics the study of ethics is often built on foundations which are not clearly connected with the earliest narratives of Jesus and of God's people.

Second, ethics at the time of these fourth-century councils was beginning to fit well into a sense of Church law, and thus would be open to the influence of legal proceedings within any of the cultures in which Christianity found itself. Roman law especially became a strong model for canon law and thus for Christian ethics. While many of the decisions reached through canon law procedures are not outside of what one might learn from the life of Jesus or the life of the early Church, both the basis on which they were argued and the procedures through which they were reached were far different. Character and virtue, truth and truthfulness became less important features than obeying the law. The Protestant Reformation accused late medieval Roman Catholicism of a works righteousness but its inheritors among fundamentalist and evangelical Protestants have been able to produce a kind of legalism which mirrors the developments that grew out of seeing ethics described in terms of systematized law.

What's the point? There is a difference between trying to remember who you are and memorizing a list of things which must be done or cannot be done. Young Christian people often know that they are not supposed to have sex unless and until they are a married couple. They know more than the Ten Commandments from their early ethical teaching in conservative Protestant or Roman Catholic homes. But when they are madly in love and greatly aroused it is a sense of who they are which can keep them out of the back seat or off the blanket. They need to remember that they not only have themselves to think about, they are part of families of character whose other members would be heartbroken with sleeping around let alone a marriage based on pregnancy alone. They are part of a Christian heritage which thinks more highly of male and female involvement in intercourse and the resultant children than a hot night or a sweet intimacy without consummated commitment would warrant. A list of don'ts won't do. It has to be identity, character within family and community. The stories behind the creed set the ethics, not a group of laws whose breaking could exact its punishment.

When these important aspects of both the council and its creed have been discussed, there is reason to take the Nicene-Constantinopolitan Creed as one small but widely accepted statement of Christian faith which can remind conservative Protestants and Roman Catholics that we are not the Denver Broncos and the Cleveland Browns or any other specific teams playing for the American Football Conference Championship. We are not competing so that when one wins the other must lose. What the creed can remind us is that we are both football teams; it is the game that matters. We are not the same and we do disagree. Those differences must not be dismissed unattended. In the final analysis, however, we have far more in common than our emphasized differences allow us to see. At the least we are all trying to be catholic Christians.

## The Nicene-Constantinopolitan Creed

We believe in one God
   the Father, the Almighty,
   maker of heaven and earth,
   of all that is, seen and unseen.

We believe in one Lord, Jesus Christ,
   the only Son of God,
   eternally begotten of the Father,
   Light from Light,
   true God from true God,
   begotten, not made,
   of one Being with the Father.
   Through him all things were made.
   For us all (humankind) and for our salvation
     he came down from heaven:
   by (the power of) the Holy Spirit
     he became incarnate from the Virgin Mary,
     and was made man.
   For our sake he was crucified under Pontius Pilate;
     he suffered (death) and was buried.
     On the third day he rose (again) from the dead
       in accordance with the Scriptures;
     he ascended into heaven
       and is seated at the right hand of the Father.
   He will come again in glory to judge the living and the dead,
   and his kingdom will have no end.

We believe in the Holy Spirit,
   the Lord, the giver of life,
   who proceeds from the Father.
   Who with the Father and the Son is worshipped and glorified,
   who has spoken through the Prophets.

We believe in one holy, catholic, and apostolic Church.
We (acknowledge) confess one baptism for the forgiveness of
sins.
We look for the resurrection of the dead,
and the life of the world to come. Amen.[8]

8. World Council of Churches Commission on Faith and Order, *Confessing One Faith: Towards an Ecumenical Explication of the Apostolic Faith as Expressed in the Nicene Constantinopolitan Creed (381),* "Faith and Order Paper No. 140" (Geneva: World Council of Churches, 1987) 7. I have adapted the wording, (men) to (humankind), and the printing of the last three clauses to reflect the threefold structure of the creed with the Church, baptism, and forgiveness, and resurrection and the life appearing under the main heading of the Holy Spirit. For a similar printing see Berard L. Marthaler, *The Creed* (Mystic, Conn.: Twenty-Third Publications, 1987) xx.

# 4

# God the Father: Maker of Heaven and Earth

The purpose of these next five chapters is to emphasize those things which conservative Protestants and Roman Catholics share in common. Differences will not be ignored, but neither will they be raised to ever greater heights. We are all Christians and that definition should take precedence over all others. To accomplish this task, I shall look at four topics set out by the Nicene-Constantinopolitan Creed and the realm of worship and life. I shall not restrict my efforts to the exact wording of the creed, but I will employ it as the base for the rest of this volume.

In that case our discussion of God turns to the first article of the creed: "We believe in one God, the Father almighty, maker of heaven and earth, of all things seen and unseen." For Fundamentalists, Evangelicals and Catholics the priority of God over everything else is part of the skeletal structure of faith. We have all learned to have no other gods before God even though all of us have found that to be more simply said than lived. The one God of Christian faith is the almighty Father.[1]

For some of us the term "father" brings remembrances of strength and authority even from experiences within our homes. Surely the word "almighty" or "omnipotent" has the sense of genuine power. Used in Greek translations of the Old Testament, the word most properly means "ruler of all." But perhaps we are also not off track when we try to envision something more

---

1. Thomas Torrance, *The Trinitarian Faith: The Evangelical Theology of the Ancient Catholic Church* (Edinburgh: T & T Clark, 1988) chs. 2 and 3.

in the phrase "Father almighty." According to both Scripture and Tradition, our Father God is no Santa Claus; his fearsome features have not totally disappeared. God's call for humans to worship, even with a tinge of fear, must not be muted because of insipid sentimentality. God does what God wills. God does not ask us what we want before God gives us what we need. It is God, the ruler of all, whom we serve, not some matchbox genie who does our bidding.

Yet from that same shared heritage we can learn that this "father" is not the drunken bum who strikes out from a raging stupor, a lout who has given the meaning to the word "father" which too many people carry for life. This is the "Father almighty" who, according to Hosea 11, has the strength and the just authority to bash Israel's people, even rip up their pregnant women. But the Father chooses another way because God is divine and not man. God taught his people how to walk as any caring father would. God watched the first steps and knew that the journey would be long and treacherous. The main characteristic of this Father is an omnipotent ruler whose steadfast love is unshakable.

Because we live in a world in which many earthly fathers have been wicked, insensitive brutes, we need to remember the patristic Tradition which warns of the difference between the "Father in heaven" and the genetic male. Compassion and sensitivity have been considered feminine virtues by a number of males within and outside the United States. They argue and act as if male virtues are something different. The "fathers" of Christian Tradition, who at times were misogynist, almost always got the following right: God the Father is not a male; "father" when used of God has no sense of gender whatsoever. It is meant to portray not only the strength and the authority, but also the compassion and sensitivity which are too often absent in earthly fathers. There is no gender in God. Gregory of Nazianzus, the second president of the Council of Constantinople in 381, thought his Neo-Arian opponents so bizarre that they might even call God male because the Greek word for God is masculine.[2] Some insist that we speak of God as "mother" in order to counter the inappropriate concepts of God which surface among our arch-conservative breth-

2. Gregory Nazianzen *Or.* 31:7.

ren, whether Protestant or Catholic.[3] In order to become better humans perhaps we need to think of God as Mother. Certainly God as male has no place in Christian faith. If, however, we inject female gender into deity because of grossly chauvinistic societal and religious practices, we compound one mistake with another. God is neither male nor female. The Old Testament stands firm against a doctrine of God which proposes characteristics for God taken from nature and goddess religions. The struggle for the equality of women, for fairness and love in the ways they are thought of, talked about and treated does not demand that the Caananite religions be reinstituted as substitutes for Christian faith.[4]

Although phrases about the Virgin Mary appear in the second article of the creed, perhaps this is the most appropriate instance to discuss her place in Christian doctrine. That has been a sticking point between Protestants and Catholics for some time and remains a troublesome issue in contemporary consultations. The Evangelical-Roman Catholic Dialogue on Mission, held from 1977–1984, raised some of the questions about Mary.[5] Evangelicals inquired about two expressions found in Pope Paul VI's apostolic charge entitled "To Honor Mary."[6] In the first when the Christmas season is described as a commemoration of Mary's "divine, virginal and salvific Motherhood," some Evangelicals asked what the force of the term "salvific" is in that phrase. The Roman Catholic participants said the text explains itself when it claims that she " 'brought the Savior into the world' by her obedient response to God's call." The second passage refers to Mary's "singular place" in Christian worship as "the holy Mother of God" and "the worthy Associate of the Redeemer." Evangelicals found the second phrase, "the worthy Associate of the

3. Among many such efforts see Elizabeth Schüssler Fiorenza, *In Memory of Her: A Feminist Theological Reconstruction of Christian Origins* (New York: Crossroad, 1983).

4. Elizabeth Achtemeier, "Renewed Appreciation for an Unchanging Story," *Christian Century* (June 13–20, 1990) 596–599.

5. "Evangelicals and Roman Catholics Dialogue on Mission," *International Bulletin of Missionary Research* 10 (1986) 11–12. Reprinted as *The Evangelical Roman Catholic Dialogue on Mission 1977–1984,* ed. Basil Meeking and John Stott (Grand Rapids, Mich.: William B. Eerdmans, 1986) 48–52.

6. *Marialis Cultus* 1974 I:5, 15.

Redeemer," questionable from the vantage point of Scripture. They also objected to a statement from the Puebla Conference on Evangelization of Latin America in 1979, which says that Mary "now lives immersed in the mystery of the Trinity, praising the glory of God and interceding for human beings." They wondered if Mary was viewed as on the same level as the Trinity or perhaps a fourth person in the Trinity.

The Roman Catholics at the various meetings of this group pointed out that the term "cooperation," when used of Mary in the Vatican II documents, may not mean a great deal more than what is found in 2 Corinthians 6:1, where humans are seen as "workers together with [God]."[7] But they called to the attention of the Evangelicals that the Magnificat in Luke 1 speaks of Mary as "highly favored" and "blessed among women." Evangelical inhibitions about the texts in Luke must be overcome if they are to follow their own concern for all Scripture. The Catholics also noted that the word "mediatrix," used of Mary from the fifth century onward, was not emphasized at Vatican II. It occurs only once in a list of titles. Indeed within the same sections Christ is twice referred to as the "one Mediator."[8]

The group of participants in their final report found that they had somewhat closed the gap between them; at least their deepest fears were allayed. Roman Catholics were uneasy with the evangelical neglect of the place given to Mary in Scripture and in the Church. And Evangelicals were uneasy about the Roman views of Mary's place in the process of salvation and were concerned about the ambiguous, in their view, misleading terms applied to her.

There are clues here for us. I do not imagine that conservative Protestants will ever view Mary as a co-mediator of salvation. They will be concerned about the background of female savior figures in Hellenistic religions. There are ways in which some clear

---

7. *Vatican Council II: Conciliar and Post Conciliar Documents,* ed. Austin Flannery, O.P., New Rev. Ed. (Northport, N.Y.: Costello Publishing Company, 1984) 28. *Lumen gentium* 56, 62, 416, 419. Perhaps the clearest clause for the distinction between Christ and Mary is in 28. *Lumen gentium* 62, 419: "No creature could ever be counted along with the Incarnate Word and Redeemer. . . ."

8. *Vatican II Documents,* ed. Flannery, New Rev. Ed., 28. *Lumen gentium* 60–62, 418–419.

borrowings from Hellenistic religions seem to have occurred in relationship to the descriptions or depictions of Mary. In early Christian art both the painted and sculpted forms of Mary breast-feeding Jesus have a strong resemblance to similar, older figures of the pagan goddess Isis. It is also not clear what effects a strong savior figure in Mary has on Christology, a topic we turn to in the next chapter. Some have claimed that the strength of Mary in popular piety may indicate a weakness of Christ.

Such argumentation from Fundamentalists and Evangelicals is not necessarily meant to be scurrilous about Mary or demeaning to Catholics. Its purpose can be primarily to raise questions about the intrusion of unchecked popular piety into the development of Christian doctrine. Roman Catholicism has been powerful in absorbing folk festivals and beliefs into the Christian faith, often changing those aspects of culture into throbbing symbols of Christianity.[9] That has been one of the victorious themes of Christ over culture. Yet at times absorbing pagan festivals has endangered the gospel. The query here is whether or not Mary as mediatrix is such a danger. Vatican II has attempted to state with some care what a proper view of Mary would be, one that recognizes the strong cult of Mary and the human example of faith which she provides.[10] With the loving assistance of conservative Protestants, perhaps Roman Catholics can strengthen the best view of the Blessed Virgin Mary within the Christian Tradition.

On the other hand conservative Protestants need to hear the corrective from Roman Catholics concerning Mary. How often is the Magnificat of Luke 1 actually mentioned in conservative Protestant churches? I can remember giving a Bible lesson on that passage in Luke, to which someone replied during the study: "That sounds Roman Catholic to me." It should. Luke was surely catholic. The Lukan text appears regularly in churches with lec-

9. *The Evangelical Roman Catholic Dialogue on Mission 1977-1984,* 73-78 noted that there is a different attitude toward culture within the two traditions, more one of continuity with Roman Catholics and discontinuity with Evangelicals. But the Roman Catholic Robert J. Schrieter, *Constructing Local Theologies* (Maryknoll, N.Y.: Orbis Books, 1985) esp. 122-143 has suggested that all Christian mission work must be much more alert to popular religion, in both its negative and positive senses, than it has been previously.

10. *Vatican II Documents,* ed. Flannery, New Rev. Ed., 28. *Lumen gentium* 52-69, 413-423.

tionaries whose biblical texts are not chosen locally. But many Fundamentalists and Evangelicals do not belong to such ordered liturgical traditions in which most if not all of the Bible is covered in a regular cycle. I must constantly remind ministerial students in my classes that they are not wise enough to choose every text which will be preached. The high praise which Mary receives within Scripture has not been taken seriously among most conservative Protestants. If they are to be true to their principle of biblical authority, they must give her more careful attention. In Luke 1 the angel addresses her as the favored one; her relative Elizabeth says she is blessed among women and Mary herself finally understands that generations will call her blessed. Without the faithful response of a virgin to the Holy Spirit, the full biblical account of the incarnation is impossible. She was that virgin. Although she wrote no gospel accounts, she is said to have "kept all these things in her heart." Perhaps the apostolic circle in some way had access to that information. She is perhaps depicted as a pushy mother in the John 2 portrayal of the wedding feast at Cana of Galilee. Yet if the silence about Joseph means his early death, she may have been almost totally responsible for Jesus' home life, in modern terms a single parent. Whether or not that is true, one point is clear. According to the New Testament texts, Mary became pregnant with Jesus without the aid of a man. That the incarnation of God as a male took place without the intervention of a male should quiet much male chauvinism which thinks of itself as Christian.

Particularly in an age when women are rightly emerging toward a place of equality, in an age when only careful exegesis of the epistles keeps Paul from appearing on the modern stage not as a male piglet but as a half-ton boar, all Christians must return with equal care to the Blessed Virgin Mary as a guide. Without loving assistance from Roman Catholics, Evangelicals will have difficulty discovering Mary's striking presence in the Scripture and her powerful example for contemporary life. If God is without gender even though referred to as "He" and "Father," and all the apostles are males, in order for the ancient truth of the gospel to make its impact in the present world, more attention must be paid to Mary and other important women in the early circles of Christianity. It will not be easy for conservative Protestants to hear that word, for male chauvinists, too, often dominate their leadership. Mutual assistance in exegeting Scripture and grasping the Tradition of the Church is crucial. Catholics also have their chauvinist leaders, but they have a much stronger heritage of female role models, starting with Mary and proceeding through the examples of many important women martyrs, mystics and saints than conservative Protestants normally have claimed.

The Nicene-Constantinopolitan Creed also refers to God as "the maker of heaven and earth, of all things seen and unseen." Those are strongly scriptural ideas which once more go back to the Hebrew Bible as much as to the New Testament. The opening chapters of Genesis and the creation psalms view God as the creator of all. The first chapter of Colossians deals primarily with Christ's participation in creation, but it emphasizes that all things "seen and unseen" are created by God. Although a number of conservative Protestants have fought against a creation *ex nihilo,* a creation out of nothing, as a traditional rather than a biblical idea, that concept does not seem far removed from the meaning of texts in the smaller Protestant canon of the Old Testament. And if one sees the phrase from 2 Maccabees 7:28 as biblical, and Romans 4:17 and Hebrews 11:3 teaching a similar view, then the position is found within Scripture itself. It was emphasized within the early Church primarily in response to a philosophical conception which viewed matter as eternal and which saw the divine maker as merely fashioning such matter into various forms. If the doctrine of creation *ex nihilo* can be asserted with proper warrants, as I think it can, it will have particular force for the materialistic age in which we live. If all things visible and invisible owe their existence to God, then they will always be secondary to God. At times in the world of conservative Protestants, it is difficult not to be overcome by the materialistic consciousness which has arisen. More than one televangelist has pushed the cause of personal materialism in a way that Karl Marx might have envied. "If you send me ten dollars, the God of glory will see to it that you receive a hundred in return. Tithing doesn't hurt. Gifts to the good cause don't cause you to suffer. God will repay." Should you find time to watch some of these particular charlatans—not all of them are— you would swear that giving to Christian causes, specifically theirs, is the best possible investment. Give to Christian missions and you will become rich. Jim and Tammy Bakker's appeals were particularly marked by such nonsense. And they got rich for a time. The economic motive dominated their lives. And now he has been in prison. Unfortunately many of the television ministries demand enormous sums of money in order that they can bring their messages to television audiences and continue to ask for more money to be on television to ask for more money. . . . They have often been so effective that there are large sums left over for colleges, hospitals and churches which tend to justify, in the eyes of some, what are too many times only afterthoughts. When you watch these people you find that they love to give you a gift for your gift. They are clearly aware that self-interest is an enormous motivator.

Only a strong, nuanced doctrine of creation can dispel those kinds of appeals and ones that are more subtle. I recently talked with a conservative Protestant couple who were appalled at the decision of their home church to build yet another big sanctuary. These two medical professionals had worked on foreign mission fields during extended vacations. Now they were attending a church which was cutting its overseas mission budget in order to erect a twenty-four million dollar building. At what point do material comforts, too often among Fundamentalists or Evangelicals referred to as "home missions," become the primary goal of a local congregation? How is the nature of the Church to be understood from a doctrine of creation that emphasizes God's absolute priority over matter?

Another subtle side of this concern can only be solved when conservative Protestants and Roman Catholics work together on the doctrine of creation as a part of the doctrine of God. How good is creation? How may material things be appropriated for human use under the almighty God? There are any number of Protestant Christians who have a certain gnostic tendency in relationship to creation. Matter is evil; it is a constant temptation. Wealth is always sinful. All bonds with the world are chains of sin. One of the reasons that certain Fundamentalists are often prone to sexual temptations along with an odd guilt and are susceptible to security-producing accumulation of wealth which does not help others in need is that they do not know how to use penultimate means for ultimate ends. They become prey to a hidden materialism because they concentrate on the ends as if any means are appropriate. Conservative Protestants need the assistance of Roman Catholics in searching for a way to understand the world as God's creation, as good, and yet still far less than the only ultimate good, God. I could chart for you some fascinating developments of churches within conservative Protestantism which started out after World War II among lower- to lower-middle-class people with little education or wealth. Now some of these folk have massive church buildings, not out of a medieval tradition in which each person built to the glory of God, but out of a subtle sense in which their own burgeoning wealth could be justified. When you belong to a church which has castigated the wealthy, and now you are wealthy—you drive the Cadillac, you live in the grand home—how do you adjust your religious convictions? Give the preacher a Cadillac at a Christmas party and see if the last vestige of his prophetic call from Amos does not disappear. Build a huge, usually artistic and architectural travesty, which matches the early Holiday Inn interior decorating scheme of your home. Tasteless but comfortable.

Fundamentalists and Evangelicals need assistance from Roman Catholics who have thought about these things for centuries. If you have not necessarily solved all those problems, perhaps you know what the pit- and pratfalls are. How can a good but marred creation be put in the service of a good God? The wealth of Roman Catholicism has been used in the construction of cathedrals, hospitals, universities, mission stations, all kinds of things which can be employed for the good of the gospel. At the same time Roman Catholic monastic orders have warned against the abuse of such wealth and have created ministries that have been both effective in terms of their results and inexpensive in terms of the funds spent on the people. As both Fundamentalists and Evangelicals in the United States acquire more funds to be dispersed, there will be a greater need to learn from the experience possessed by Roman Catholics, both good and bad.

Because I am a Tennessean who was asked to speak about conservative Protestantism and is now focusing on the doctrine of creation, I cannot avoid the topic of creationism. Much like the theme of inerrancy, creationism is difficult to discuss because so much folly has been involved. Fundamentalism was making remarkable strides in winning its battle with Modernism in the 1920s until the Scopes trial in Dayton, Tennessee. William Jennings Bryan, one of the first great communicators and indeed a friend of Clarence Darrow, was made to look a fool. Bryan thought that his ability to speak well from the stump would serve him in a courtroom, but when he agreed to take the witness stand, he became playdough in Darrow's hands. He could not make the details of Scripture fit exactly—because they don't—and he did not know either the details of evolution or the import of its positions. Cartoons abounded in the press; buffoonery triumphed. Bryan died soon after the trial and the Fundamentalist cause was seriously wounded. During the 1930s Fundamentalists were often perceived as closely related to monkeys if not baboons.

Many assumed that the picture of an inerrant Scripture, describing in historical detail the creation of the world, had been destroyed and would never return. But life is bizarre. People who did not respond favorably to a number of developments within the modern world found solace in Churches which stood on the infallible Bible and attacked the moral decay of contemporary life. Thus in the last two decades a number of southern states have attempted to pass laws which demand the teaching of the biblical account of creation alongside of the evolutionary account. The great constitutional battles took place in the 1970s in Arkansas, but less than a decade ago a Fundamentalist mother, named Vicky Frost, won a lower court decision against the school board of Greeneville, Tennessee—some thirty miles from my home—when she insisted that the school did not allow alternative texts for her children to study. A higher court has overturned that decision and Tennessee's secretary of state ruled in August, 1988, against yet another attempt to create a bill which would require the teaching of biblical creationism alongside evolution.

In many ways the issues have not significantly changed from the 1920s. For the conservative Protestant, God's creation of the world, when coupled with an inerrant Scripture interpreted in a flat, literal manner, cannot allow evolutionary developments. In the 1800s when dinosaur bones were discovered and Neanderthals reappeared, conservative Christians at times called such things hoaxes. Some, like the Piltdown man, evidently were. Occasionally popular books will emphasize that same hoax aspect of contemporary science.

But a new tack has been developed. Now creationism is no longer developed so firmly from a biblical base over against science. Its proponents want it to be viewed as a science within the scientific community. They see evolution as one scientific theory among many and offer the biblical view as another scientific theory which should be given equal time. This tack has had a certain amount of success. It does not need to argue that the Bible is *the* Word of God or that it is an important document in Western culture which should be included in the education of any human being. The initial argument would most probably be refused in pluralistic communities in the United States because it would stand against the freedom of religion stated in the first amendment of our constitution. The second would be relegated to history or sociology classes and not placed within the science curriculum. To put the biblical view of creation within the science curriculum as a scientific theory alongside other scientific theories is at the least an interesting project.

It rests upon some rather fascinating observations. As Walter Cronkite once noted in a television program about the Leaky family, the unique fossil evidence of the development of humankind could probably all be placed in one rather small room. If the evidence for the lines which did not lead to humankind are excluded —using the most recent anthropological and paleontological assessments—that is probably true. Any curious human should be excited by what has been found but also a bit skeptical of the sweeping charts based on such small amounts of evidence. That skepticism can come from someone with atheistic or agnostic views of God and little interest in religion; it need not be limited to Christian believers.[11]

But those defects in the programs of evolutionary theorists are not strong enough to turn away the attention which must be focused on the defenders of creationism. First, as a number of rather level-headed people have indicated, creationism is a pseudoscience. I have not been particularly taken by Carl Sagan's sweeping claims

11. Michael Denton, *Evolution: A Theory in Crisis* (Baltimore: Adler & Adler, 1986) apparently has no religious axe to grind. He is, however, a sharp critic of the lack of evidence for evolution's largest claims.

aided by colored television sets, "billions and billions" and all. But he is probably on target when he notices that creationists' dependence upon the Russian maverick, Velikovsky, is at best misguided. Velikovsky developed a theory of catastrophe within the history of the universe so that its age could be calculated at about 10,000 years rather than the "billions and billions" which our scientific communities regularly assume. Velikovsky's position, or something similar, is rather widely held among creationists and is an odd one indeed. In the seventeenth century bishop Ussher calculated the age of the earth on the basis of the apparent biblical chronology at 4004 years. My assumption is that his figures are relatively correct if one assumes that biblical "years" are like our calendar years. But now you will often find the 10,000 year figure in creationist literature because it comes from what can be considered a "scientific" alternative. This is an interesting tip. The actual texts of Scripture are not now as important to the semischolarly debate as is the construction of an alternative scientific explanation. Exact correlation with the Bible is not as significant as is the view that creationism is a science.

Some quackery is involved as well as no small amount of ignorance. I once listened to a defender of creationism talk about the brilliance of God's creation of humankind by describing the joints of the hand and the remarkable properties of our skin with its hair follicles. I leaned over to a friend of mine and said that a gorilla would have made an excellent example for the points taken. But quackery is not one-sided on this issue. Supporters of evolution need to confess their sins as well. Human skulls have been faked; dating methods have proved incorrect. Theories have become dogma without the care and questions of Darwin. We need to be warned about the difficulties on both sides of this issue.

What puzzled me about the speaker who defended creationism was not that he had compartmentalized his thoughts about science but that he could not see the problems involved with his public arguments. What was of most concern to me was that he misrepresented both the views of modern evolutionists and the texts of the Bible. Stephen J. Gould, a Harvard paleontologist, took a trip to Tennessee to see the site of the Scopes trial. He also has taken the time to read some of the best representatives of creationism in the contemporary period. Although I would like to see some of his positivism humbled in light of recent philosophical discussions of epistemology and would be more impressed if he acknowledged the weaknesses of even improved evolutionary theory, I do appreciate his clear response to the creationists. He notes that many of them are fighting Darwin and have not made themselves aware of the changes in modern evolutionary theories. That is a fair charge and one that indicates part of the problem with creationism. In too many cases it does not know its enemy. It has not taken the time to see that Gould and others are not teaching exact Darwinism. Gould claims that he has been misquoted and misunderstood on important points. He is correct.[12]

But more important for me as a conservative Christian is that the bulk of the people involved in these debates are not very good students of Scripture. Many of the defenders of biblical creation have not read their biblical sources. As a scriptural theme, creation is not restricted to Genesis 1 and 2. If one stays for the moment with the accounts in Genesis, it is clear that both chapters do not say exactly the same things. In chapter 1 the creation of Adam and Eve is last; in chapter 2 it stands first. Chapter 1 does not say how humans were created; chapter 2 offers a series of pictures that give God hands and have God use earth and God's breath to make man. Chapter 1 describes a process spread over six "days"; chapter 2 does not. Chapter 1 gives no specific location for the place where the male and the female were put; chapter 2 names them Adam and Eve and places them in the garden of Eden.

The usual picture of biblical creation that one learns in early childhood is a collage of these accounts. A number of conservative creationists are troubled by biblical scholarship which has called attention to these details and thus views the creation account as unhistorical and mythical in the sense of untrue. But the differences of detail remain no matter what explanation one gives to the accounts. Furthermore, the creation psalms which deal with

12. Stephen J. Gould, *Ever Since Darwin: Reflections in Natural History* (New York: W. W. Norton & Co., 1977) devotes at least one essay to the oddities of Velikovsky, a "scientist" who is often used as basic by creationists. Gould, in his *Hen's Teeth and Horses Toes* (New York: W. W. Norton & Co., 1983) devotes three essays to creationism, one which takes to task creationists who have misrepresented his views and another which recalls with words and pictures his visit to Dayton, Tennessee, the site of the Scope's trial.

the same themes make no attempt to describe creation in the same detail found in Genesis. They can speak of land as beams, the heavens as a stretched tent, and the clouds as chariots: all images which are not used in Genesis. They do not always find it important to mention Eden. In Ezekiel 28 when Eden is mentioned in a tirade against the king of Tyre, the place is described as being dominated by a mountain at the time of creation, and the people there being clothed with or having skin of jewels rather than any kind of nakedness. Those features are certainly not found in Genesis.

The saddest aspect of most creationist literature is that it does not represent the fullness of biblical creation accounts. Rather it defends a child's picture of creation with descriptions which are not faithful to the rich and variegated images in Scripture. The Bible's lack of unified details concerning how creation came about, its varied pictures of God's creation of all things, visible and invisible, are seldom if ever given their due. A Fundamentalist or Evangelical effort to describe creation over against evolution as some kind of alternative scientific theory fails because it is neither fundamental nor evangelical. When Scripture is read selectively and thus restrictively, the project is not biblical. The only way to understand the biblical view of creation is to let the passages that speak about that theme tell us what they will in their own context.

The great confession of these texts is that God is the creator. But in witnessing to that they make use of different pictures of how God went about that task, ones which seem to be borrowed from the creation motifs of other cultures and religions as well as contemporary acts of creation such as erecting buildings. Taken together these rich descriptions of the process can be seen as totally contradictory and thus destructive of a singular doctrine of creation or they can be seen as uninterested in a consistent description of *how*. In either case their differences cannot be denied. If the Bible is not interested in one exact description of the *how*, then it is appropriate for a contemporary Christian to listen carefully to different descriptions of how this world came to be and developed. No view is likely to be Fundamentalist, Evangelical or catholic which does not see God as the creator. But the biblical lack of concern with a consistently described *how* stands against any defense of creationism as a doctrine of the Church.

The Bible and Christian Tradition show great interest in *why*. Scripture and Christian Tradition see purpose and reason in the universe. Twentieth-century science is often uninterested in the why. Stephen Hawking, the great English physicist, is at work with many others on a full explanation of all reality, an attempt to develop an overarching theory of reality which will include both Einstein's and Bohr's theories. He seems most optimistic about the possibility of results. For him the universe will end up being a boundless, closed system which will explain itself. When the theory appears we will know what God knows.[13]

Officials of Roman Catholicism have been quick to endorse some of these new theories, perhaps in an attempt to soften the problems of the Enlightenment or particularly the checkered history of the Roman Church's reaction to Copernican theory. Sadness over that affair is to be applauded. But we will have to hear more from Hawking and his colleagues before their views can be squared with Christian revelation. For the average reader like myself, the place of God seems to be more like that suggested by the physicist Laplace: none at all. In any case, Fundamentalists, Evangelicals and Catholics do share a belief in one God, the almighty, creator of heaven and earth, of all things visible and invisible. No matter how we are pressed properly to give up chauvinist conceptions of life, subtle dependence upon materialism, and visions of the scientism called creationism, we may respond through the ecumenical tradition about God which we have received from Scripture and from Tradition. We need each other's different viewpoints to see with more than one eye. But in order not to be parochial, we will also need to remember that Christians who do not claim to be Fundamentalist or Evangelical Protestants or Roman Catholics would affirm what the Nicene-Constantinopolitan Creed says about God. In order for us to be evangelical and catholic they must also be our discussion partners.

13. Stephen Hawking, *A Brief History of Time: From the Big Bang to Black Holes* (New York: Bantam Book, 1988).

# 5

# Jesus Christ: True God Become Man

The bulk of the Nicene-Constantinopolitan Creed, as well as much of the New Testament, is concerned with Jesus Christ. In the rather standard printing of the creed, twenty-one of the thirty-four lines deal with him. The article concerning God the Father is a background for all that is said of Christ. In the Hellenistic context it needed to be stated since a belief in one God could not be assumed in 381. Julian, the emperor for a time in the 360s, tried to revive polytheism and had only minimal success perhaps because of the brevity of his reign. While at Antioch of Syria he remembered the great pagan festivals of the past which had honored Apollo and prepared to attend such a noisy, crowded occasion. But he found not only that the temple was in disrepair, but also that the priest and he were the sole worshippers for the day. Instead of the throngs of people and the scores of animals to be sacrificed, the emperor looked on the single priest who had brought a small goose from home. Yet Christians across the empire were frightened by Julian's attempted restitution of government support for the old polytheistic rites. Paganism was much stronger in places other than Antioch. Believers in Christ seldom if ever thought of Christian faith without its claim of monotheism.

It is the place of Jesus, however, which is dominant. The better theologians among conservative Protestants recognize the charge of Christomonism raised against some of their number. There is among certain Fundamentalists and Evangelicals a unitarianism of the second person of the Trinity. We all need to learn of the Son by looking to the Father. Without the Hebrew

Bible, Christianity is inexplicable. But it is still the case, as the New Testament claims and this creed indicates—by emphasis if not by content—that we learn the nature of the Father by looking to the Son. It would be impossible to explain the sense of Christian faith if all references to Jesus Christ were removed.[1]

This does not mean, however, that Christ has been understood in exactly the same way by all people within every age. The purpose of this creed was to call those of different views back to the fold or to exclude them if they persisted in their opinions. The opponents most often in focus within this creed were the Neo-Arians led by strikingly intelligent and educated theologians like Aetius and Eunomius, mid-fourth-century philosophers of religion who considered themselves Christian. Following up on the Alexandrian Arius' early fourth-century insistence that the Son was not of the same divine nature as the Father, and perhaps that Christ did not have the full human nature which we do—no human intellect or will—the later Arians formed worshipping communities who still found their center in Jesus Christ. They could honor him in worship, a worship which they would not give any mere man. Various fragments of their works show that they could poetically confess that Jesus Christ was not like any other creature. But they worked diligently to protect the monotheistic understanding of Christianity against the pagans by clearly distinguishing between the Father and the Son. They also developed a different understanding of salvation in which, as a second-level divine figure, Christ could more readily identify with and be an example for human beings.

For the later Arian philosophical theologians like Aetius and Eunomius, the important thing was to discover the exact name of the Father and the Son so that the character of each could be deduced logically from that name. In their view the proper name of anything revealed its essence. Names were not merely convenient approximations; they were God-given revelations of the nature of things. Thus if God's name was unbegotten, and the

---

1. The most Catholic and catholic Christology written by a conservative Protestant comes from Thomas C. Oden, *The Word of Life: Systematic Theology, Vol. 2* (San Francisco: Harper & Row, 1989). Oden has mined the nuggets from the fathers of the Church, particularly concentrating on the first thousand years. His work is destined to be a classic.

Son's name was begotten, they could not be of the same divinity because their names were direct opposites. This kind of thinking is difficult for us to accept in our age of advertizing. Usually when a product appears in the marketplace, it will soon be "new" or "improved" or in the "economy" or "giant" size. My favorite at present is a cereal called "Just Right." I recently purchased the "new larger size;" I'm waiting for new, improved "Just Right." We correctly tend not to trust names and know they will change.

The Nicene-Constantinopolitan Creed's article on Jesus primarily has later Arians in view. Jesus is Lord, the only begotten Son of the only God. Neo-Arians would have no difficulty confessing that. They worshipped Jesus as Lord and insisted that unlike any other creature he was the only begotten Son of God. But they resisted the claim that the Son was "eternally begotten of the Father" or that he was *homoousios* with, "of the same essence" as, the Father. For them the Son was begotten before time began and thus did not belong to those creatures fashioned within time. He was no average creature. But in their view a point existed when God was not Father, when God was only the unbegotten one. God began to be a Father when God had a Son.

Much of this was heavy going for someone listening to a lecture after eight in the evening and may not be much easier for you the reader. But the issues perhaps are clearer than we sometimes allow them to be. Those who constructed the Nicene-Constantinopolitan Creed wanted to make clear that the bulk of their confession could be directly reproduced from Scripture. In 1 Corinthians 12:3 and other places Paul referred to Jesus as Lord; John 1:18 called him the only begotten Son of God. In John 8:12 Jesus says he is the light of the world; in 1 John 1:5 God is called light. Certain translations and punctuations of Romans 9:5 and 1 John 5:20 refer to Jesus as God and true God. With little or no dispute most readers see that John 1:1 says that the Word was God, that in John 20:28 Thomas cried out to Jesus, "My Lord and My God," and that Hebrews 1:8 indicates the Son is God.

Within writings outside the creed, defenders of a Nicene-Constantinopolitan theology claimed and interpreted the passages which were fundamental to the later Arian views. The man Jesus was made Christ as Peter said in Acts 2. According to Psalm 8 he was like other humans: highly regarded and thus a little less than God. The Son as the first born of all creation was that one of whom Colossians 1:19 also said "in him all the fullness of God was pleased to dwell." Nicenes insisted that their views were more inclusive of Scripture's wholeness than were those of the later Arians. They could attribute the weaknesses of Jesus to his humanity or his limitations as the Incarnate One and predicate the strange and miraculous powers of his divinity. In their view, the later Arians were never able to account for the biblical passages which indicated that Jesus the Son was God.

Supporters of Nicene theology found Arian Christology to be subtle, but inappropriate. It sucked the life out of the Son's divine place. But when it came to creating this creed, they were puzzled about how to approach such a sophisticated sense of language and theology as the Arian philosophical theologians had produced. So they reached out to words and concepts beyond Scripture to make their own meaning clear. The only Son of God was "eternally begotten of the Father." "Before all the ages," before time, he was there as Son. They could again employ Scripture, John 1:3, in placing the Son within the creation process, "all things were made through him." But eventually they stood upon the Nicene rock of the *homoousios* to make their message clear. The later Arians were capable of wrenching nearly every piece of Scripture into a system that made a certain kind of persuasive sense. But there were still those pieces in Colossians 1 "in him all the fullness of God was pleased to dwell," in Philippians 2 "he did not count equality a thing to be grasped" or in John 1 "the Word was God," or in John 14 "he who has seen me has seen the Father." These poetic passages, the Nicenes thought, had their true meaning expressed within the confession of the *homoousios,* in a contemporary term which insisted that the essence of the Father and the Son is the same.

It should not be too shocking that contemporary conservative Protestants have as a rule continued to claim the Nicene-Constantinopolitan Creed as their own in the midst of their usual insistence upon the priority of Scripture over later tradition. Even with its pivot on a nonbiblical word, they find in this creed a center which, as they see it, Scripture itself demands. In their struggle with what they call the inheritors of American modernism of the

1920s and the classical liberals of the late nineteenth century, conservative Protestants often found solace in this ecumenical creed. It is tradition, but it is Tradition which expounds Scripture. It reflects the interpretations of John's prologue, Thomas's confession in John 20, Hebrews 1:8 as well as 1 John 5:20, Romans 9:5, Colossians 1 and Philippians 2 which they depend upon. It is Traditional Christology that was securely in place within the magisterial Reformation, found in both Calvin and Luther. Trinitarian theology is no newcomer to fundamentalist or evangelical circles. They have battled the so-called "liberal" interpretation of these passages in Scripture, and have taken to task some of their own who have questioned whether or not the earliest Christian communities within their Jewish context could possibly have claimed that Jesus was God.

Many fine Roman Catholic scholars, biblical specialists, historians of Christian doctrine and systematicians, have questioned the possibility of such biblical claims. The winds of freedom which have blown through the stately old structure of Roman Catholicism have encouraged much searching and questioning, and rightfully so. But from the standpoint of Fundamentalist or Evangelical Protestants, attempts to diminish the full divinity of Jesus Christ violate the nature of Christianity. Battles with liberal Protestants have not made it easy for conservative Protestants to support fully the struggles of Edward Schillebeeckx or Hans Küng. Küng has been viewed by Evangelicals as thoroughly instructive on the doctrine of the Church when he has resisted papal infallibility. But his Christology and his views of resurrection have not been well-received among Evangelicals. Schillebeeckx has been given a similar treatment primarily because conservative Protestants insist that he has taken too many liberties with the biblical texts in his espousal of modern interpretative methods. Yet I doubt that any Evangelicals will be pleased with the reaction of Lefebvre and his supporters, for their stand seems to be much more conservative in terms of the priority of Roman tradition than conservative Protestants could accept. There will continue to be ambiguous reactions by Fundamentalists and Evangelicals to these developments within Roman Catholicism: pleasure in the weakened hold of tradition on Roman Catholicism and an increased dependence upon the Bible but sadness and caution in the acceptance of a kind of historical-critical biblical study which displaces one of the Church's foundation stones like conservative Christology. Cardinal Ratzinger, no welcome guest in every conservative Protestant or Roman Catholic home in his position as the inheritor of former inquisitorial power, was asked by evangelical Protestants to give the Erasmus lecture at New York in 1988. Within his lecture he called for careful hermeneutical studies which ask historical-critical questions of historical-critical method. That was his message to Evangelicals.[2]

Fundamentalist and Evangelical Christologies are often difficult to separate at least in the sense of their ultimate positions. Fundamentalists put forth inerrancy of Scripture as basic and will usually attack and then ignore most if not all historical-critical investigation of Scripture. Evangelicals often question how historical-critical the present methods of scriptural study are, while trying to stay abreast of the developments. Fundamentalists attack Roman Catholicism as a dastardly distortion of Christianity, some accepting the view that to be Roman Catholic is not to be Christian.[3] Evangelicals usually receive Roman Catholics as cousins with a different set of diseases. Thus Fundamentalists and Evangelicals can be distinguished on some counts. But in Christology they are quite similar.

They believe as the Nicene-Constantinopolitan Creed and Scripture state that Jesus Christ was born of a virgin, that he became incarnate by the Holy Spirit. Much ink has been put to paper in defending the traditional view of the biblical accounts. In the midst of all that paper it is important to remember that Fundamentalists or Evangelicals do not believe in the virgin birth because they avoid participating in the modern world. Rudolf Bultmann was incorrect to think that those who turn on light switches will be forced to reject such ancient confessions. Some conservative Protestants have made it a point to work through assumptions of modern

---

2. See Joseph Ratzinger, "Biblical Interpretation in Crisis: On the Question of the Foundations and Approaches of Exegesis Today," *Biblical Interpretation in Crisis: The Ratzinger Conference on Bible and Church,* ed. with a foreword by Richard John Neuhaus (Grand Rapids, Mich.: William B. Eerdmans, 1989) 1–23.

3. Jimmy Swaggert, *Catholicism and Christianity* (Baton Rouge, La.: Jimmy Swaggert Ministries, 1986).

science to a view which is opposed to logical positivism. They are not convinced that all reality can be verified or falsified empirically. They are not persuaded that art, poetry, and music are basically nonsense. Of course, one does not have to be an empiricist or a logical positivist to find a conception like virgin birth unbelievable. But it is also the case that one need not be anti-modern to suggest that such language within the community of faith is not to be discarded on the basis of the most rigid, parochial understandings of contemporary science. I have a friend, Lawrence Schaffer, who is a noted physicist in the field of materials testing. He has created a number of tests to determine what kinds of compounds would work best as the lining of atomic reactors. When I talk to him about an overview of physics, he is impressed by how much the field has reduced its organizing concepts from well-defined and interlocked laws to a small group of strong principles. Outside those principles much is unknown and within the realm of possibility. There are certainly those like Stephen Hawking and his impressive circle who are looking for a unified theory, a singular explanation of everything. But others like my friend are hard-headed "Missouri mules" who are not as convinced a unified theory is possible and find Hawking a bit too trusting in his hope for human progress. Within that context one who believes in Jesus' virgin birth or his resurrection as events that occurred need not be completely ridiculed as one who is out of step with any reasonable sense of scientific reality.

Yet some of the silliest paragraphs I have ever seen have been attempts to demonstrate that virgin birth and resurrection are possible by proving that they have happened elsewhere. The better part of conservative Protestant thought on these issues voices its puzzlement over one major assumption: that the scientific community has so firmly defined reality that anything Christians have traditionally termed "supernatural" or "miraculous" is impossible. Some Fundamentalists will reject any attempt to run Scripture through the colander of modern reality as an attack on the primacy of Scripture. But some from the evangelical camps will question whether or not it is reasonable to be so certain that any modern sense of reality must deny the possibility of such events. Others within both groups will also call attention to the sense that Scripture itself seems uninterested in great mythic structures and puts together virgin birth, crucifixion, death, burial, and resurrection in the same type of narrative structures it uses to depict any historical events.

I well remember a discussion of resurrection at a working group on theology in Tübingen, Germany, in which a professor of New Testament made this last observation and was ridiculed by a professor of systematic theology as if he were a Neanderthal. Out on the edges of evangelical Protestantism, where labels are not claimed but positions are shared, there are imposing figures who are not certain that either Scripture or creed should be stripped of references to virgin birth and resurrection, particularly not on the basis of modern conceptions or an apparent dependence on ancient mythological structures. Some are insistent that the Jewish background of the New Testament has given it a character in which it wants to report such stories as actual events.

It is this kind of commitment to the centrality of Jesus Christ's divinity in both Scripture and Tradition which led to the remarkable outburst over Scorsesee's film, "The Last Temptation of Christ." Fundamentalists, Evangelicals, and Roman Catholics picketed the film and called for its destruction. Apparently Bill Bright of Campus Crusade for Christ, a conservative Protestant group of considerable influence, tried to buy the film so that it would never be shown. I would not be surprised if some in the audience when I gave these lectures and some of you as readers were offended by the force of this conservative reaction, wondering both if it made any sense and if it did not call attention to the movie far beyond anything which the studio could have done to advertise it. Few films have the whole religious section of *Time* magazine devoted to them.

That movie hit a nerve. Many conservative Protestants and Roman Catholics usually are prepared to concede that Christians have failed. The query "Why would I want to join a bunch of hypocrites like you?" hits home. But deep within the Christian community is the sense that Jesus Christ was different. He was tempted in all ways like we are, but he did not sin. He who did not sin was made sin for us that we might be freed from the full effects of our failings. Depict that central core as questionable and you get visceral reactions. I continue to be embarrassed by the weakness of some arguments mounted by those who picketed the film, but I am neither surprised nor in essential disagreement with the sensitivity which stands behind it. If Christ was seldom if ever certain of who he was, if he was a vulnerable fellow who possessed a bunch of neat tricks like taking his heart out of his chest, but was not the divine savior of the world, then something basic and necessary to Christianity has been ripped out.

Much of my own aversion to the demonstrators is that they felt called by God to insist that the film not be shown, when they probably should have used the film as an entrée to discussions about who Jesus Christ was and is. I have had wonderful talks with young people about who Jesus is, talks prompted by their viewing the film. But it is the lack of sensitivity from Christian critics of the film which I find abhorrent, not their deep and abiding sense that if Jesus was just a regular guy like other interesting people, except that he could do some wild tricks, Christianity is no longer Christianity. The film itself was rather boring and crude. I went to sleep. I was awake for the sequence in which Jesus apparently dreamed that he impregnated Mary Magdalene. He also dreamed that God caused her to die before the child was born. I turned to my friend and said, "At least the death of the child may keep them from making the sequel, Son of God II." Had a film of this quality been made about Napoleon, few would have bothered to view it. Although some of the individual performances were admirable, the film as film was often artless. The special effects of "Star Wars" were far superior.

Yet many conservative attempts to make films of Jesus' life have been rather vulgar in ways this one was not. They make Jesus look absolutely inhuman, at times even inhumane. Both Scripture and Tradition, particularly the Council of Ephesus in 431 and the Council of Chalcedon in 451, the latter with its Chalcedonian Creed, well indicate that some Christians have had a problem with the humanity of Jesus. Biblical scholars concede that the details of Jesus' life and teaching do not amount to a biography in the way we usually understand that genre. As a conservative I am not impressed with the insistence that we do not know much more about Jesus' actual life than what the creeds tell us: born, crucified, died, buried. The narratives as we have them in the gospels did reach their final form after the resurrection event, something I hold to have happened. But I am not convinced that there was a resurrection plot or that what was written after the resurrection so changed the material from before the resurrection that none of it is trustworthy as a depiction of Jesus himself. Too often modern scholars without much sense of or appreciation for oral traditions have insisted that all was changed after the Church began to believe that Jesus was raised from the dead. A former colleague of mine who grew up in Canada told me a modern story which gives some sense of how historical details can stay in place even in the midst of passing decades. Years ago he went with his grandfather to water the oxen at a large trough. When he asked about the trough, his grandfather told him that it had been hewn from one large tree by the boy's great-great-grandfather. In passing on the information the grandfather was covering four generations in one telling. We must be careful not to minimize the fault of memory and the lack of interest in exact detail found in Synoptic or Johannine depictions of Jesus. But we also must not be overcome by a rather silly sense that anything retold after twenty-five or fifty years and then written down must be suspect in every detail.

If there is a rather trustworthy anecdotal retelling of Jesus' life in the gospels, framed within theological concerns but still not without historical interests, then we can say more things about the human Jesus than the creeds confess. And if we look at the gospels themselves we will find not only stories about the miraculous deeds of one who was anything but the average human being, but also anecdotes about one who was quite human. Growing up in a preacher's home I memorized a good bit of Scripture when I was young. At church we also had various contests for children, ones in which memorized Scripture gained you points. Not being completely stupid, I quickly got a few points by reciting the shortest verse in Scripture. "Jesus wept." Five points for Norris.

Although in contemporary theology with its sense of God's suffering, we need not see that verse as restricted to the human nature of Jesus, it certainly is a human emotion. I also doubt that Jesus turned over the tables of the money-changers without some adrenalin flowing and some anger involved. To claim that he was never angry appears to be more the creeping-in of a stilted piety from certain eras of Roman Catholic as well as Victorian Protestant faith. Part of the white women's burden during the Victorian

era was not only putting up with sex, but also seldom if ever show-
ing anger. Although those stereotypes have been destroyed as ex-
planations for a whole era, my maternal grandmother thought
faith called her never to be angry or in despair. Thus she would
have accepted some of the strange exegesis of Psalm 22 and Jesus'
most poignant cry from the cross. "My God, My God, Why hast
thou forsaken me?" In too much conservative piety, whether Protestant or Catholic, faithful people have had difficulty seeing either
rushing despair or fiery anger in those words. Yet without such
emotions the cry is senseless. Jewish piety has been marked, not
merely by Teviah in "Fiddler on the Roof," with a sense of questioning prayers. If God is omniscient, if God does know all, why
do we think God will never know our despair and anger as long
as we don't mention it?

I also suspect that Jesus had a developed sense of humor that
has been almost forgotten or covered over by a rather rancid piety,
one that grew in the various cultures that have nurtured Protestant Fundamentalists and Evangelicals. Such a dismissal of humor can also be seen from Roman Catholic sources. In the Desert
fathers almost all laughter is rejected as frivolous or ridiculous;
it is a form of deep temptation from the Devil. My own bias in
favor of humor must be made clear. My father's family in particular is noted for its raucous practical jokes. I learned laughter
so well from my Dad that we have been mistaken for each other
when the booming guffaws erupt.

Yet there are places within the gospel accounts of Jesus which
a stern, scowling interpretation subverts. Much effort has been
made to explain how, according to Matthew 19, a rich man might
get into heaven if he had as much chance as a camel getting
through the eye of a needle. Perhaps you even own a one-volume
commentary or a Bible dictionary which speaks of the gate called
the eye of the needle, one which a camel could crawl through on
its knees if pulled and pushed by its owners. But what if Jesus'
words were a good joke, one understood by those poor and down-
trodden folk who so often had ears to hear his words. I do not
doubt that some people of wealth could enter the kingdom. The
gifts from the rich women described in Luke 8, ones who supported Jesus' life, seem neither to have been refused by Jesus nor
ridiculed by Luke. In another instance Jesus told a particular rich

man to sell all he had and the poor fellow went away sad because
he had so much and loved it so deeply. It is still the love of money
which is the root of evil. But some of the parables have a sense
of irony or humor, an odd and unexpected view which calls staid
common sense into question.[4]

If you approach the gospels with a smell of life on your breath,
with a glint of fun in your eye, you find a Jesus who could spin
a good tale, could attract strong and earthy followers as well as
the cultured, and had a range of emotions worthy of any full
human being. You may have found Scorsesee's film portrait of
Jesus offensive. Perhaps you took the advice of friends or leaders
you trust and have not seen the movie. But there is no reason at
all that you should either start or continue to read the gospels
as if Jesus had no human life whatsoever. Scorsesee's film says
it does not follow the gospels; it doesn't. But many other films
of Jesus' life make him into a cardboard pietist who wouldn't
know a joke if he heard one. (I know a preacher among our
churches whose parents named him Ivan when his last name was
Odor. "Ivan Odor" as your name on a grade school playground,
means Jesus' humor got lost on those parents. They must have
been fine, upstanding people to raise a young boy who went into
the ministry, but surely they had tin ears when it came to school-
yard fun.)

The stories both about Jesus and the ones he told of others are
filled with life. All of us as Christians will continue to be seen
as decidedly odd if our piety is devoid of such energy. We have
not fully grasped the great mystery of Jesus' person, described
in the ancient Church as one person in two natures. Who he is
has often been plumped from the stump, but never plumbed to
the depths. Yet clearly the denial of his divinity is no worse than
the denial of his humanity. As that early Church, which all Christians share, often said with sharpness, we are not saved unless
he was both fully God and fully man.[5]

---

4. Elton Trueblood, *The Humor of Christ* (New York: Harper and Row, 1964)
discusses a number of passages that may depend upon humor.

5. For a remarkably clear treatment of the "theandric union" of Christ, that
he is one person, fully human and fully divine, see Oden, *The Word of Life,*
165–169, 197–203, 527–534.

For Fundamentalists and Evangelicals salvation is often described primarily in terms of substitutionary atonement. The Nicene-Constantinopolitan Creed emphasizes that the Son descended from heaven because of humans and for our sake died, rose and ascended. Christianity without a sense of sin and salvation would be strange indeed. Since some Christians tend not to speak of sin, I merely remark that their position is decidedly odd. To say that Jesus took the place of the sinner, that he who knew no sin became sin for us, involves much of the apostle Paul's doctrine of salvation. He emphasized that all have fallen short of the goal, and that all stand in need of salvation in Christ. In Romans 2 he gives more than a passing nod to the great moral attainments of pagans who have lived according to their own sense of values and who might be excused in the judgment. But in fairness to an incomplete aside, I do not find it likely that he proposed a way of salvation which was outside the work of Christ. Certainly among both fundamentalist and evangelical Christians the sense of the need for Jesus' blood sacrifice rests near or at the core of their beliefs. Conservative Protestant hymnody is filled with references to such Biblical descriptions and concepts: "power in the blood," "washed in the blood," "for me he died." I dare say that any study of Roman Catholic piety with its sacrifice of the Mass, with its hymnody and art centered on the crucifixion, has many of the same features. Again this is one of our deeply shared aspects of Christian faith.

It is unlikely that even on the basis of a quantitative analysis of Scripture much would be left of a description of salvation if substitutionary atonement were dismissed. Yet the gruesomeness of that depiction has certainly not gone unrecognized. Questions have been asked in many ages of Christian faith concerning the shedding of blood, the character of a God who would demand payment. At best substitutionary atonement presents a stunning picture of the significance of sin. Those of us who are apparently well-educated and cultured, who deplore the slaughter house but love the meat, who give to the hospital drives but find the operating room revolting despite its healing, are not well-suited to grasp this old, central metaphor. We too often demonstrate that we have outgrown life. Something with blood and guts exists for an auto mechanic or a soldier, but not for the rest of us. Yet birth, healing and death are messy. To use the kindergarten word, a lot of life is yukky. A yukky atonement fits.

It is sad, however, that more of the classical metaphors for atonement do not mark conservative Protestant or Roman Catholic doctrine. They do at certain points but they have not penetrated far enough into the center. Following Jesus as an example pales before a blood-filled sacrifice. But there are numerous biblical passages in which being a disciple of Christ depicts how to get on with the Christian life. Although technically salvation can be described as available to all in the death and resurrection of Jesus, in his act of atonement, we do ourselves no favor if we cut any cords that would tie Jesus as moral example to our understanding of salvation. From what we know of him, he is worth following. And it is rather silly, although perhaps logically valid, always to distinguish between salvation and sanctification, between Christ giving his life and our living the Christ-like life as if somehow that distinction must be an unmanageable gulf. If following Jesus is bootstrap salvation—watch me lift myself—it presents dangers. But if too much emphasis is given to objective salvation accomplished by God in Christ, moral responsibility can be given a death blow. Perhaps we should keep Jesus' example before our eyes as one way of talking about salvation, not merely sanctification. Both Scripture and patristic Tradition see it that way.

A conservative Protestant or Roman Catholic sense of salvation in Jesus Christ might also be adjusted biblically and traditionally by paying more attention to another metaphor of salvation which is indeed mysterious. John 10:32-25, used to support biblical inerrancy on the basis of an aside, actually stresses that Jesus quoted Psalm 82:6 in response to Jews who wanted to stone him for blasphemy. They were appalled at his claim to be the Son of God; he noted that Psalm 82:6 calls people gods and thus that his claim was not without scriptural context. Although the incident is in some ways a cryptic one, Jesus accepted Psalm 82:6 as saying: people are gods.

Paul in 2 Corinthians 8:9 offers a picture of salvation which was to provide motivation for giving funds to Macedonian Christians in need: "For you know the grace of our Lord Jesus Christ, that though he was rich, yet for your sake he became poor, so that by his poverty you might become rich." The metaphor is not explained; it is set directly in the context of the appeal for money. But that image suggests that the richness of Christ is seen in his divinity and his poverty in his humanity. Therefore, the result of salvation in its ultimate sense is that Christians will share in the riches of Christ's divinity.

Such an interpretation of Paul's metaphor stands in line with 2 Peter 1:3-4 where the author says that the faithful may become partakers of the divine nature and escape the corruption of this world if they hold true to God's power in Jesus Christ and rest on the promises given them. It was fashionable within many Christian circles in recent years to speak of Koinonia groups, communities of fellowship and deep caring. But the author of this passage speaks of such participation not in each others' lives, but in the divine nature.

Eastern Christianity, particularly in Irenaeus (a missionary to France in the second century) and Athanasius (a rather frequent Egyptian exile to Germany in the fourth century) has shared this doctrine of *theosis,* "divinization," with the West. Gregory Nazianzen, one of the three hierarchs of Eastern Orthodoxy, presented a developed picture of Christology and salvation along these lines. In order for believers to become gods, the divine Son must assume an entire humanity so that our entire humanity may become divine. Protestants, both liberal and conservative, have had great difficulty with this teaching. They have been so overwhelmed by the distinction between God and creation that they have found the biblical warrants for this position flimsy and the developed Eastern Orthodox doctrine both materialistic and degrading. Harnack, in his great *History of Dogma,* described the teaching of *theosis,* "becoming gods," as a clear example of the Hellenization of Christianity, its diversion into strange and mistaken channels.[6] In the nineteenth-century translations of the Greek Fathers into English, this aversion to their views led to some funny adaptations. As you may know some rather risqué descriptions of sexual practices were left in Latin within these English translations so that only the properly educated could read them. But in this instance a nice trick of English was employed to soften a differ-

6. Adolf von Harnack, *A History of Dogma.* Trans. from the 3rd ed. by Neil Buchanan (New York: Dover Publications, 1961) Vol. 2. [Vol. 3], 288–304. [The Dover ed. is 7 volumes in 4.]

ent view. When a Greek patristic writer said that we shall become gods, the English translation sometimes reads not the nominative plural but the genitive singular. Thus the Greek Father is made to say, not that we shall be divine, but that we shall belong to God, become God's. Certain Protestants and Anglicans could stomach belonging to God, but not becoming divine.

The scriptural passages which support this view are few and decidedly unusual, but they are attributed to Jesus and Paul, not just to the possibly late epistle of Peter. Furthermore there is in this doctrine of *theosis* a powerful symbol of the mystery of salvation. Whatever the life eternal may be, it will not be limited to the golden streets and precious stones described in the Book of Revelation. In terms of some fundamentalist or evangelical popular piety, it will not be merely a matter of sitting on a log somewhere in a pleasant meadow and talking with friends—even Paul and Jesus—about all those questions not answerable here. If this doctrine of salvation is correct, a much greater, an inexplicable event, is in store. We shall be partakers of the divine nature. Words fail and mysteries appear.

Such views of soteriology, the doctrine of salvation, should be important to Christians. This latter view of *theosis,* becoming participants in the divine nature, introduces the subject of eschatology, the doctrine of the last things. In Christian faith the Lordship of Christ and his judgment of the world form an analogue with his place with the Father before the beginning of time and his participation in creation. Certainly in the eyes of many Roman Catholics these are views shared with conservative Protestants. Within the modern world, however, many have found them ludicrous or immoral. How can one speak of God's kingdom in light of the empirical reality of evil? What is the point of judgment when there is no clear sense of life after death of any kind?

No logically invincible answers emerge to those questions. As Christians we live from faith to faith. But perhaps some attempts shared by both conservative Protestants and Roman Catholics are in order. I have never been able to understand the force of the Christian message when it is stripped of its sense of incarnation, resurrection, and judgment. To say that God rules, that the kingdom of Christ has no end, and at the same time to deny a sense of afterlife with fair and gracious judgment by a righteous judge seems odd. In our daily affairs we know that forces clearly recognizable as good lose many battles. At best we sometimes see our lives in the fight against evil as the boulders which line the Cleveland harbor. The waves of Lake Erie will eventually destroy the stones, but without the stones nothing stands in their way. Furthermore, we are not granite but limestone, watersoluble to a frightening degree. If there is no settling of accounts, if there is no way in which more peace and justice may appear than what we now see before us, why should we use such words? We ourselves know that more content should be available. Any gospel, any good news worth its salt, should confess it.

As the educated and cultured we always want to be tolerant and understanding. As Christians we are taught to be forgiving. But surely the Holocaust, and the many genocides somewhat similar to it in Turkey, parts of Russia, Cambodia and indeed the slaughter of Indians in our own country—ones which do not take away from the Holocaust's horror but only deepen our sense of how often humans reach such depths—should make us aware of the need for some sense of right and wrong. Stanley Hauerwas, an ethicist at Duke, sometimes responds to his students who ask if any ethical absolutes exist: "It is wrong to stick a rubber hose into someone's intestines and fill them with water until they explode in order to gain information." For shock value he colors the language a bit. But it is odd that we live in such fear of proclaiming kingdom and judgment that we fail to find any absolutes at all. When did grace become so cheap, justice so far removed from mercy? Perhaps we watch too much television, too many movies in which the bad guys wear black hats and can be overcome with such ease. Blinded by such trivial stories, consequent evil becomes unrecognizable.

In Detroit a few years ago during a struggle over control of the cocaine traffic, a group sent gunmen to annihilate a rival. They killed him, his wife and five children. They did not kill the eighteen-month-old infant because she could not speak to identify them. No more force than necessary. I have played a dramatic game called Persecution with high school and college-age young people in which roles are assigned: some as Christians, some as Roman soldiers and magistrates. At the completion of one game in which I had been cast as a magistrate responsible for public order and had sent a group of Christians to their death, one young man was astounded that I had him killed because he was rebellious. We Christians who deal with power or evil in this world, particularly consequent evil, must take care to understand what we lose if we deny either the ultimacy of God's kingdom or the judgment of Christ. For many conservative Protestants and most Roman Catholics Christian faith without such understandings is better not referred to as Christian faith. We believe in incarnation, resurrection, judgment, and life eternal because we know the power of evil, not because we live as if it did not exist.

Christians known either as Protestant Fundamentalists or Evangelicals or Roman Catholics find a center in Jesus Christ, both divine and human in one person, who was born of a virgin, lived and taught among humans, was crucified, buried, and resurrected. He cried, laughed, got angry: all without sin. He was one with God, active in creation, came to save us, returned from the dead, will judge the living and the dead, and will never cease to be Lord. People who approach him may come because of their sense that he is divine and otherworldly or that he is the finest human being they have ever read about. Either way the center of his person and work is both/and, not either/or.

# 6

# The Holy Spirit: Giver of Life

The Nicene-Constantinopolitan Creed contains a group of short phrases about the Holy Spirit: "the Lord, the giver of life, who proceeds from the Father,[1] who with the Father and the Son is worshipped and glorified, who has spoken through the prophets." They are rather small ones given the debate which must have surrounded their inclusion. Gregory Nazianzen, the second president of the Council of Constantinople, had noted in sermons preached during 380 within the city that some called the Spirit God, while others refused such terminology as blasphemous and still others allowed the thought and accepted the claim in silent prayer, but not in public worship.[2] Modern discussions of the Holy Spirit also involve lively debates although the points at issue are quite different from those of the fourth century.

The 1960s and 1970s produced a number of political and social upheavals in American life. When these lectures were given at John Carroll University the traveling monument to the Vietnam War dead was on campus. As a nation we have not yet found

---

1. Most students of Church history now understand that the debate between Eastern Orthodoxy and Roman Catholicism about the procession of the Spirit, the *filioque* controversy, should be decided in favor of the Eastern position. The original text of the Nicene-Constantinopolitan Creed mentioned only that the Spirit proceeded from the Father, a reflection of John 15:26. It would be of no service to Christian unity for conservative Protestants and Roman Catholics to agree that the Spirit proceeded from the Father *and the Son,* and in the process offend the Eastern Orthodox.

2. Gregory Nazianzen *Or.* 31:5.

an appropriate way to take in all that war or those decades meant to us. In terms of American religious life, the 1960s and 1970s also marked a rather fascinating upheaval within congregations, one particularly characterized by personal renewal and the so-called charismatic movement. Many Churches, both Protestant and Catholic, have not learned exactly what to do with that movement. Yet the charismatic phenomena are clearly one major feature of any look at the Holy Spirit among Christian communities although they are not mentioned by the Nicene-Constantinopolitan Creed.

Certain attitudes and actions of devout conservative Protestants and Roman Catholics that are associated with the Holy Spirit may give one pause. In the eighteenth century Joseph Butler wrote to John Wesley, "Sir, the pretending to extraordinary revelation and gifts of the Holy Ghost is a horrid thing, a very horrid thing." Although at present the so-called charismatic movements within various Christian circles are not receiving the press coverage which they did in the 1960s and 1970s, there are Christians in many denominations, not just among Pentecostals, who rely heavily upon the Holy Spirit, particularly as that Spirit guides them in the utterance of prophecies, in the speaking of tongues, and in the interpretation of those tongues. For any of us who do not participate in these activities—I do not—there are a number of reactions. A kind of shock occurs when people begin what they call "speaking in tongues" and others start to "interpret those tongues." For many who make their own decisions without God, or those who reach decisions with God's help in some other form, such experiences appear at best quite odd and at worst quite mad. But often those perceptions are in the eye of the beholder.

In the 1960s I was a young preacher in Oklahoma, serving within a town of 116 people and 5 churches. The Christians in the region often attended each others' yearly revivals. That allowed me the privilege of attending my first Pentecostal meeting. Since so many of those services are very informal, I was not surprised to be asked, after I had entered the small building, if I would lead the group in the evening prayer. I was escorted to the platform in the front of the church and took my seat beside the preacher. At the appointed time he motioned that I should lead the group in prayer. When I opened my mouth it seemed that everyone in the meeting burst into loud prayers of their own. I had been thinking so hard about what I might say in my prayer which would lead to a better understanding between those of us in the Christian Church and these in the Pentecostal Church that I was stunned when I found out no one would be listening. Then my sense of humor kicked in and I wondered how they would know when I was finished. I continued my prayer to what seemed to be an appropriate length. As I got nearer the end I noticed that the din of voices was beginning to subside; each prayer was becoming softer and softer. As I droned on in the rather hymnic phrases which end preachers' or priests' prayers, the room was almost silent, so that when I said the Amen, in unison they said it with me.

This was an experience I would not soon forget. But more was yet in store. Although I have a raucous sense of humor and, at least as a child, had disrupted my share of public meetings and church services, I was offended at the lack of "order" in that revival. I had been taught the lessons of decorum well in my youthful days. When my best friend and I were in junior high we went to a piano concert, seated ourselves in opposite halves of the audience, and on the count of synchronized watches, began to yawn endlessly. Just as one of our teachers had said in an aside, yawning was an almost irresistible suggestive device. Two junior high boys were able to ruin a concert of over a thousand people. But our fathers grounded us and thus ruined our next set of plans. I learned then not to brag about our feats with my bedroom door open. And I also learned that there was a kind of structure for public events which should not be broken. I had already discovered some of the limits of the spiritual order necessary for church services after I hit my father in the face with a paper airplane launched from the balcony. Somehow he thought that disrupted his preaching. Thus when I came home from the Oklahoma Pentecostal meeting I was convinced that those Pentecostals had no sense of decorum. They should read Paul's first letter to the Corinthians, particularly chapters 12–14 where he talks about doing things decently and in order. Why should they pray out loud when *I* was leading in prayer?

The next year at the Pentecostal meeting I was taught a humbling lesson about their practice of everyone praying out loud in different words at the same time. Since I had been asked to lead in prayer the previous year, I was not the honored guest at this service. I sat in a pew with my wife. Behind me sat one of the biggest men from our area. My memory may fail me, but I remember him as at least six feet four and over two hundred and fifty pounds.

We had a general store in that town where you could eat a great country-style meal for next to nothing, browse around, or play checkers. You might just drink a cup of coffee and talk. Except for the race of planting and harvest, life never moved too fast. And most men would find some way to spin yarns or color the news in ways which did indeed remind you of Will Rogers. But that great big fellow seldom if ever said a word. I had spent an hour or two at a time in that store when many of the men were there and had never heard him utter a syllable.

That was true when he was relaxed; it was also true when he was angry. We had so few children among the 116 people that eventually the state took away the accreditation of our school. The district was to be broken up and the children bused other places. Messing with their children makes parents uneasy and feisty. Even worse our district had oil revenue and all the other districts lobbied to get that even if they had to take the kids. At the town meeting this huge fellow became so angry that he got up and walked out through a row of chairs. That made a lot of noise as you can imagine, but it was more exciting because people were sitting in some of those chairs, or at least they were before he came through. On his way out he never said a word.

But that night in the Pentecostal meeting when it came time for those inappropriate prayers, the disorder which I knew was improper, my big neighbor grabbed the pew in which I had been sitting and made it shake with his strength and energy. The calves of my legs were against it and I could feel it vibrate. When the prayers started, he spoke. He prayed a prayer so beautiful that to this day I remember the lilting sound of his voice and the vibration of that pew. When everyone stopped, he stopped, probably never to speak in public again until that little Pentecostal church all prayed aloud together. And I went home chastised with a much deeper sense of dignity and decorum.

Whatever you think of Pentecostal experiences, I hope that

these stories have given you some sense of how the apparently strange practices can fit the needs of some people in ways that my usual practices cannot. You will find some charismatics who demand that all speak in tongues in order to be saved. But during a six-month interim of preaching for a Church of God I learned that about half of their members had never spoken in tongues. Furthermore, a woman who was a Pentecostal tongue-speaker once said to a friend of mine that he would never need to speak in tongues because he was such a fine public speaker. There is no monolithic position taken by fundamentalist or evangelical Pentecostals, as I am sure there is none among pentecostal or charismatic Catholics.

A group of rather carefully researched positions must be recognized, perhaps even conceded if both your personality and your heritage, like mine, have not led you to value these experiences. First, there is no direct correlation between these activities and a particular personality type or socio-economic level. Tongue-speakers and tongue-interpreters are neither always bizarre, nor always people with psychological distress, nor always poor. They cannot be dismissed as the fringe element you must anticipate finding in any group. They also do not belong wholly to the lower economic and social classes of any society. I have personally known some of them who were well-educated, marvelously creative and economically successful people, who in ways inexplicable to me found solace and strength in these exercises.

Second, psychological or sociological categories cannot be used to explain away these kinds of experiences without consistently denying the possibility of any mystical, otherworldly acts. Most Christians, even some fine Roman Catholic philosophical theologians like Louis Dupré of Yale, have argued that any fair description of human experience must include a place for the mystical.[3] Given the sense of the supernatural in Christian Scripture and Tradition, many are hesitant to rely upon a reductionistic perspective which rejects all such events, including miracles and resurrection. But at the same time others are hesitant to seek after special gifts or experiences as the ultimate manifestations of the

3. Louis Dupré, *The Deeper Life: A Meditation on Christian Mysticism* (New York: Crossroad, 1981).

Spirit in the present era. How do we remain cogent and critical while making allowances for events not fully subject to what we learned in school as encompassed within natural law? How do we believe the gospel and avoid the charlatans who prey upon our beliefs and push us toward embarrassing gullibility? These are not easy questions, for they cannot be answered by removing all sense of unusual events. Yet we will be wise to be cautious. It is not realistic to exclude the unusual without some kind of evidence, but neither is it realistic to give it credence without some kind of evidence.

Third, charismatic phenomena do not appear only in Pentecostal groups; they also have found their way into the highly structured liturgical traditions like those of Anglicans and Roman Catholics. One respected historian of Christian missionary endeavor, Walter Hollenweger, a professor emeritus from the University of Birmingham in England, has suggested that such experiences will be a significant aspect of ecumenical Christianity, of World Christianity, within the next millennium. As Christianity grows more rapidly in the southern hemisphere of our globe, and continues to be marked by these features, Christianity has and will become much more "pentecostal".[4] Here in the United States and in most northern countries we shall have to rethink what these phenomena of the Spirit are and how they fit into the Christian life. Some of you and I do not seek such manifestations or find them within our own communities, but our views do not necessarily demand that these gifts are bogus, or that they should never exist among us. We must be watchful, but also recognize that within World Christianity as a whole such phenomena are far more usual than they probably are among run-of-the-mill conservative Protestants or Roman Catholics.

Fourth, neither Scripture nor Tradition demonstrates that these phenomena are nonexistent or heretical in every case. Few of us would doubt that there has been a kind of quackery involved in certain situations. At a pentecostal service I once attended, the minister's daughter began to speak in tongues. She had led the singing and was on the platform with us. As she walked to the front of the podium, others joined her, both speaking in some

4. Walter Hollenweger, "After Twenty Years' Research on Pentecostalism," *Theology* 87 (1984) 403–412.

different language and interpreting the tongues in English. Suddenly she stopped her speaking in tongues, came back to me and asked if I would be willing to be the speaker at a meeting the following month. I could hardly believe that she was making the request just then, but I agreed; she returned to her place, and began again to speak in tongues. Her experience was obviously no uncontrollable trance, no possession by any spirit, and her timing did not make it easier for me to believe in her practice.

Yet if one looks at the Scripture and the history of the Church there have often been genuine experiences of the Spirit among Christian people. In 1 Corinthians 12-14, my scriptural passages for order and decorum, Paul is concerned both that the abuse of the practice be stopped and that the phenomenon not be excluded. He would rather speak in intelligible languages than many tongues in need of interpretation, but he strongly warns the Corinthians not to forbid speaking in tongues. Although some of the fathers of the Church appear to be limiting such experiences, or at least claiming that those experiences have subsided in their time, careful research usually indicates that these experiences have existed to some degree in each age. The two dangers seem to be either claiming that every Christian must have one of these gifts, especially speaking in tongues, or that any who do have them must be either demon-possessed or insane. The appearance of tongues can bring with it these two extremes. I know a fine conservative Protestant pastor who in one congregation first angered a particular group because he could not find scriptural warrants for excluding tongue-speakers from the fellowship. A group who opposed charismatic gifts as demon possession left the church. Later the pastor angered those he had defended because he would not follow without question the prophecies one of their strong leaders was receiving "directly from God," prophecies which demanded that the church take a particular view of its future. Anyone who went against the prophecies was against God. Those who believed that way then left the church.

These are not easy questions nor will they be answered in any balanced way without a great deal of personal and communal pain. I do not know of any better advice than that which was offered by Paul in 1 Corinthians 12-14, but his affirmation of such experiences and his insistence that all gifts of the Spirit serve the edification of Christ's body, the Church, is not easy advice to follow. Christian love is not something you fall into because the manhole cover is loose.

Graciously most of the scriptural metaphors concerning the Holy Spirit are not limited to a discussion of spiritual gifts. John 15:26–16:15 has Jesus say that he must go away before the Comforter or the Counselor can come and lead believers into all truth. Those are daring words. Without context they well might mean that Jesus was an incomplete savior, a figure who only initiated the salvation of humankind, but by himself could not finish it. A more attentive reading makes it clear that Jesus is encouraging his disciples by indicating that his own divine presence in the Spirit will not leave them desolate. They may indeed expect to be comforted and encouraged by the Holy Spirit who will lead them to understand even more about the gospel than they grasped when they were with Jesus himself. Obviously those words are meant to be heard by disciples well beyond the apostles, those who had never seen or heard Jesus but could expect guidance and support through an indwelling Spirit. Many pious Christians take that promise at face value, as a twofold description of words said to the apostles and phrases meant for them. Although highly charismatic Christians may find special meaning in those words, particularly when set in the context of prophecies given for guidance to the contemporary community and individuals, all Christians find in them a certain comfort, if a certain uneasiness. Surely the Spirit is alive and well and living somewhere not limited to Argentina.

On a negative note, many conservative Protestants have grown up within the warning that the sin against the Holy Spirit is the one unforgivable sin (Mark 3:29). When revivals were a rather common fare for those who enjoyed public speaking as entertainment if not as Christian preaching, one night would be devoted to the unpardonable sin. Even in my younger days, well beyond the time when revival meetings were the most successful tool of mass evangelism, I can remember such sermons. Sin has always been a preoccupation of conservative Christians, both Catholics and Protestants. But perhaps I can fairly say that few sermons other than the gory descriptions of Christ's death could so captivate a guilty conscience as one on an unforgivable sin. Although

I cannot remember the answers given in the few times I heard such sermons, I can recall the utter terror which they more than once provoked.

A proper exegesis of that passage still escapes me. Even a look at Thomas Aquinas' catena on the gospels does not bring much enlightenment. But one thing is certain. No conservative Protestant treats the Holy Spirit as the wastebasket of theology, the place where the trash belongs. I do not know if I could have grown to appreciate the great positive passages within Scripture concerning the Holy Spirit had I not had a bit of "consciousness raising" in those younger days. Modern Protestant Evangelicals will as a rule leave the surging sermons about the unpardonable sin to the Fundamentalists, but no Evangelical known to me will approach a doctrine of the Spirit with yawns of indifference.

Other biblical passages also find prominence. Romans 8 with its sense of the activity of the Spirit in prayer nearly always plays a significant role among conservative Protestants. Prayer is a staple of their life. Therefore Paul is encouraging when he says that the Spirit enables us to pray even when we do not know what words to utter, when all we can do is feel the numbing pain. Protestant Fundamentalists, Evangelicals and Roman Catholics find comfort in the claim that the Spirit intercedes and makes known to the Father our deepest longings. This rather stunning promise finds expression in many Christian books on prayer. That promise is filled with hope, for much more often than some staunch Christians might want to admit, we do not know what we should pray. When my father's father was dying of cancer, we all wished for healing, but also hoped that the suffering would subside if need be in death. How many times in the life of a believing Christian are we faced with choices in prayer which go far beyond our ability to know what we should ask?

This understanding of prayer becomes most instructive because there is a type of prayer, highly developed among some charismatic Protestants, that has a tendency to overstep the bounds of humble faith into the arena of presumption. Friends and acquaintances of mine have described how they have worked diligently to create what is referred to as a fleece. Coming from a family with a raucous sense of humor I have been struck by the odd play on words that this use of language creates. Fleecing God, whether it be the Father, the Son, or the Holy Spirit, seems too comical for serious consideration. But the background of this terminology is the Old Testament story of Judges 6:36-40 in which Gideon put out his fleece as yet another test to see if God really wanted him to lead Israel in her battle with the Midianites. Although all Fundamentalists or Evangelicals would not lead a prayer life organized primarily around the fleece, some quite pious conservative Protestants find this kind of prayer appealing and warranted. The point of the exercise is to lay such a clear question in prayer before God that whatever happens will indicate his will.

During the energy crisis some years back an engineer had a brilliant and workable idea for the creation of energy reservoirs. His concept was not suited to every region, but the geological formations necessary for it were available in a group of major urban centers within the United States. He applied for a patent on his concept and received it. A large corporation wanted to pay him in order to implement his idea; they would pay well and the applied concept would have helped in the energy crunch. After thinking over the offer, and praying about it as any devout Christian might, he constructed a fleece. On a particular morning, if he received three phone calls at his home where he had his office, he would make the deal with the corporation. If not, he would refuse. He did not get three calls; he rejected the offer, and he felt that he had followed the clear will of God in the decision.

I was puzzled then by the action, and continue to be unclear how that practice can be squared with Paul's promise that the Holy Spirit will mouth our unspoken prayers when we cannot put them in words. Knowing the exact will of God for a given event through a constructed fleece has given me pause. How do I distinguish it from magic? Shouldn't a Christian's careful evaluation of the situation, surely under the leadership of God and in the prayer of the Spirit, be the process for making decisions? This type of piety offers secure answers for those who find the process convincing, but it raises questions about how one can appropriate the fleece without being fleeced or fleecing God.

Surely one of the strongest reasons why many fundamentalist and evangelical Christians think of the Holy Spirit as on a level with the Father and the Son is the involvement of the Spirit in salvation. Paul in 1 Corinthians 6 talks about the Christian being washed, sanctified, and justified in the Spirit of God. For conservative Protestants a Spirit-less Christian faith is dispirited indeed. My sense is that something similar marks most Roman Catholics when they are called upon to speak about the Spirit. They might not go directly to each of the biblical passages mentioned here, but they would likely arrive at them if by a more traditional route, that is, through Church Tradition.

In the undergraduate class I taught at John Carroll University on televangelists, we watched a tape of a sermon by Jerry Falwell. He told the story of a man dying of cancer who wondered if he had really been saved. Now that he was on the verge of death, he needed some answers and telephoned Falwell. Falwell explained to him what he called the plan of salvation, particularly what the new birth of faith would be. He wanted to make certain that this fellow was "born again."

As Falwell made clear in the rest of his sermon for that Sunday, all people are mired in sin. In his view all humans have inherited our fate from our original parents, Adam and Eve. Even though the first humans were made in the image and likeness of God, they fell, they lost their inheritance, and passed the fallen condition on to us. Only by the grace of God, only by being born of the Spirit, being born again by God's divine activity in us, can any of us be saved. For many Fundamentalists and Evangelicals, Jesus' death on the cross paid the price and purchased our salvation. But that salvation comes to us, takes root in us only when we are born again, when we are born of the Spirit.

Although newspaper articles have picked up the phrase "born again" as a term of ridicule for Fundamentalists and Evangelicals, both within Scripture and Tradition there is the sense of the Spirit as the giver of new life. John 3:3-4 talks of being born of the water and the Spirit. The Nicene-Constantinopolitan Creed says the Spirit is the life-giver. Few who have in some way experienced such new birth would have difficulty making sense of that creedal phrase. Fundamentalists and some Evangelicals have at times put so much emphasis upon the necessity of being born again that they have invited the ridicule of the media. But it is difficult to imagine a Christian who does not live in the power of the life-giving Spirit. What we often argue about are the terms of that birth, and its consequent life. People of different personalities will react to these truths in different ways. Adults who had never before experienced the powerful release which comes from accepting forgiveness of sin and newness of life in Christ Jesus can often identify the exact day or hour in which that reality struck them. The fundamentalist televangelist Jerry Falwell refers to the exact time and place when God's grace burst into his life.

Part of this conception is tied to an understanding of Christian response based on adult conversion and adult immersion. A great number of those participating in mainline Protestant churches and almost all those involved in Roman Catholic parishes were enfolded into the faith as infants. The renewed emphasis on evangelism and the Rite of Christian Initiation program for adults has begun to change that situation for Roman Catholics. But many Catholics were infants when their godparents were selected and a symbol of God's grace was administered by the Church in which a baby without its own decision was viewed as a member of Christ's body on earth. Confirmation classes around the time of puberty are often used to enhance an early baptismal event so that the baby who is now a youth may make his or her own decision. But it is a difficult procedure. The old Augustinian sense of original sin injected into the human race by the fall of Adam and Eve, the sense of all humans being sinful because sexual conception is itself sinful, still lurks in the background of infant baptism, and is often found to be wanting by Protestants and Catholics alike.

I suspect as an outsider looking in on such traditions that the enfolding of young children from Christian families into the faith occurs far more solidly as those children watch the actions and attitudes of their families than in some irreversible act which occurs when they are baptized as infants. In my tradition, which relies on adult immersion, there is an increasing sense of how important it is to acknowledge that babies growing up in Christian families within a congregation are in a dramatically different situation from babies in non-Christian homes. A number of our churches have ceremonies during the year, usually for a group of young babies, in which their parents and the congregation are admonished to take seriously the teaching ministry we have before these little ones. No adult immersion tradition which takes its responsibility seriously should overlook that sense of things, a sense of the power of the Spirit in the witness of the community.

Yet there are other problems within that tradition. I was baptized at seven, old enough to know right from wrong, but not by any means an adult. I insisted on my immersion in the presence of parents who were not in favor of it at that time. Thus in many ways I have grown up within the Church almost as a Roman Catholic or mainstream Protestant might, quite dependent in my development toward Christian maturity upon my family and the Church. When those of us who have grown up within the Church are called upon to experience a revitalizing new birth or a terrifying old fear for our salvation, we have difficulty responding. Yet as I mentioned earlier, I lost nearly all semblance of faith during my early seminary years and had to work my way back, first into the circle then on toward its center. Because of my own life's journey I have a sense of both sides of this particular issue. Christians can grow in faith on a rather steady course directly from their earliest childhood experiences into adult decision to continue the course. But those who have had that gradual development should be neither insensitive to nor unkind toward those who come to faith in fits and spurts. Our world is filled with nominal Christians who could profit from a revitalized connection with the life-giving Spirit. Perhaps some of the discussions which take place on the basis of chapters such as these could be how Protestants or Roman Catholics can respond to those within their midst who have profound, world-changing experiences of the Spirit and want to talk about them with old Christian friends. For them, something new and vital has occurred. At times when they talk, they almost burst with a sense that all Christians surely must share such experiences.

I once sat in the home of a man who had been a rather nominal Christian and was healed from a debilitating injury. One of his knees had been locked since surgery in high school, not totally stiff but quite restricted in movement. At a neighborhood prayer and Bible study meeting, led by Pentecostals devoted to a healing ministry, his knee unlocked. He built the muscles back by riding a bicycle and working out with weights. But he knew what that knee had been like before, and what it was like then. When I talked to my friend, he wanted me to share that sense of power and vitality which had come into his life. I tried to do that, for my parents had been told when I was a second grader that I would be dead in 72 hours from the polio that was attacking my central nervous system. I believe firmly that the prayers of Christians helped me live. But try as I might, I was never able to share completely the total reversal which the healing and the power of the Spirit had meant to that man and his wife. I regret that, but do not know how I would have changed it. We sometimes border on being separated totally by the way in which we experience the faith, something heightened when it is the apparent activity of the Holy Spirit which is involved.

Those who have experienced this power of the Spirit in their lives, in conversion, in healing, or in special gifts like speaking in tongues or the interpretation of tongues, must themselves remember that the work of the Spirit is not limited to such activity. The Apostle Paul in Galatians 5 well reminds us that there is fruit of the Spirit—as opposed to works of the flesh. This fruit is love, joy, peace, patience, kindness, goodness, faithfulness, gentleness, self-control. Those virtues appear among Christians who have never experienced a wrenching conversion nor a mighty manifestation of spiritual gifts. And they grow directly from the Spirit. Our task together as Christians is to find ways in which we can live together in the Spirit on the basis of quite different experiences without finding fault with each other to the point of separation.

That task is one which not only conservative Protestants and Roman Catholics must face in relation to each other. Among Protestant Fundamentalists and Evangelicals there are also those who insist either that people must have these experiences or that they are out of order. Some, who would demand that one be born again, would deny any other manifestations of the Spirit. Among Roman Catholics it is not always easy to get charismatics and non-charismatics to recognize each others' virtues.

We must also see other activities of the Spirit in places that those who are most often talking about the Spirit sometimes miss. Particularly within the book of Acts, the Spirit is viewed as that divine force who breaks down barriers between races and classes. At Pentecost when the Spirit filled the speakers and they spoke in tongues, those from Judaism outside Palestine were confronted with a message which called them to participate in full (Acts 2). Squabbles between Hellenistic and Jewish Christians over the unequal treatment of widows demanded the attention of leaders "filled with the Spirit" (Acts 6). Samaritan half-breeds burst into the Church through activity attributed to the Spirit, delayed perhaps to teach the Jerusalem disciples that those they considered to be racial mongrels were not outside the pale (Acts 8). Finally the Spirit pulled full Gentiles inside after it worked diligently to change Peter's views (Acts 10). As a Tennessean friend of mine once remarked, the Spirit is a wall-buster. The Holy Spirit cannot stand walls which divide people from each other because the Spirit knows that all people are God's creatures.

Similar to the apostles of old, we in the contemporary Church have much to learn from the Spirit in that area. Social reform or social action is too seldom seen by some conservative Christians as a work of the Spirit. Yet interestingly, it is precisely the Pentecostal and Holiness groups within conservative Protestantism who have often been at the forefront of crusty issues like slavery and women's liberation. The lack of social consciousness which forms some definitions of Fundamentalists and Evangelicals perhaps better fits the followers of Old School Presbyterianism than Pentecostal or Holiness people who have frequently battled for the rights of the oppressed. And in the persons of mystics like St. Teresa of Avila and St. John of the Cross Roman Catholics can look to saints of the Church who had special experiences of the Spirit, taught ascetic practices and worked to reform their orders in ways which led to social reform. Indeed among both Protestants and Roman Catholics it is not only exhilarating experiences of the Spirit and a wealth of virtues, but also a life of active wall-busting which is one mark of the Spirit. To evangelize is Spirit led; to heal is Spirit led; to be virtuous is Spirit led; but so is living an active fight against racism, against the oppression of the poor, against cultural or educational walls which keep us apart. Perhaps we have ignored the field of social reform, never allowed it to come home to us as a Christian task, because we have too seldom talked about it in terms of the Holy Spirit. Somehow we need to find common ground which will allow Protestants and Catholics to bring their mutual strengths to bear on such issues.[5] Talking about them as tasks of the Spirit rather than entirely under the rubric of ethics gives the discussions new force.

Much of what I have described here may seem strange to you. There are, however, some ways in which conservative Protestants and Roman Catholics share similar views of the Spirit. The bulk of conservative Protestantism is firmly Trinitarian as is Roman Catholicism, although Evangelicals, much like the so-called fathers of the Church, often depend on direct Scriptural exegesis for that position more than some groups of Roman Catholics do. Unlike the old saw concerning mainstream Protestantism, the accusation that it has made the doctrine of the Holy Spirit its wastebasket— what doesn't fit elsewhere can be disposed of there—most Fundamentalists and Evangelicals have a deep sense of the importance of the Holy Spirit. That often begins with the recognition of the many ways in which the Spirit is given an important place within the Scriptures, particularly the New Testament. The so-called Great Commission of Matthew 28:18-20 links all evangelistic efforts to baptism in the name of the Father, the Son, and the Holy Spirit. Because conservative Protestants are marked by their interest in world evangelism, they are drawn to this verse and thus to a baptism which includes the Spirit. Although most of them do not employ the threefold form of immersion as the Eastern Orthodox do, and many use some form of pouring or sprinkling, they usually invoke a threefold formula at the time of baptism. As Roman Catholics respond to John Paul II's call for renewed evangelism[6] and work through the Rite of Christian

5. Vatican II specifically pointed out areas of social concern in which Catholics and others could work together. See *Vatican Council II: The Conciliar and Post Conciliar Documents,* ed. Austin Flannery, O.P., New Rev. Ed. (Northport, N.Y.: Costello Publishing Company, 1984) 32. *Unitatis redintegratio* 12, 462–463. The organization *Evangelicals for Social Action* seeks similar goals.

6. John Paul II, *Redemptoris missio:* On the Permanent Validity of the Church's Mandate, Encyclical Letter December 7, 1990 (Washington, D.C.: Office for Publishing and Promotion Services, United States Catholic Conference, 1990). Also see *Heritage and Hope, Evangelization in the United States: Pastoral Letter on the Fifth Centenary of Evangelization in the Americas, National Conference of Catholic Bishops, November 1990* (Washington, D.C.: Office for Publishing and Promotion Services, United States Catholic Conference, 1990).

Initiation classes for adults, this Trinitarian sense of baptism will itself be reemphasized.

Conservative Protestants also rely upon a series of biblical passages which mention God, the Son and the Spirit. The prayer of Paul at the close of 2 Corinthians (13:13) is threefold: "The grace of our Lord Jesus Christ, and the love of God, and the fellowship of the Holy Spirit be with you." In 1 Corinthians 12:4-6 Paul uses the same kind of cadence: "Now there are varieties of gifts, but the same Spirit, varieties of service, but the same Lord; and there are varieties of working, but it is the same God who inspires them all in every one." 1 Peter opens by identifying its addressees as "the exiles of the dispersion . . . chosen and destined by God the Father and sanctified by the Spirit for obedience to Jesus Christ." Jude 20 admonishes Christians: "Pray in the Holy Spirit; keep yourselves in the love of God; wait for the mercy of our Lord Jesus Christ unto eternal life."

There are many twofold confessions within the Scriptures, ones which mention the Father and the Son, or God and Jesus Christ. That is the most frequently attested pattern in the New Testament. Paul opens most of his letters with a phrase like "grace and peace to you from God the Father and our Lord Jesus Christ." Over the years, a number of arch-conservative Protestants have refused to use Trinitarian language partly because of the impression these twofold formulae have made upon them. They have been quite willing to see Jesus Christ as God in the flesh, but referring to the Spirit as God has been difficult for them. They have precursors in the history of the Church. Basil of Caesarea, a fourth-century stalwart in the defense of Jesus' divinity, never referred to the Spirit as God and never accepted for use in public worship the philosophical language about the Spirit's sharing the same nature as God the Father. He was willing to think such thoughts, and even to pray silently with the divine Spirit's aid, but he could not bring himself to speak of the Holy Spirit as God.

Nevertheless J.N.D. Kelly, an expert on Christian creeds, notes that at least thirty-two times within the New Testament the three-fold pattern is evidenced. Furthermore it never appears in places where the context forces its inclusion; a twofold mention of Father and Son could have been used had it seemed most appropriate.[7] Thus even Fundamentalists or Evangelicals who are reticent about Trinitarian Tradition in early creeds or Church Tradition must acknowledge that these passages about God, Christ and the Spirit are themselves imbedded in the New Testament; they are not added to it. As I have taught these things myself at Emmanuel School of Religion, a conservative Protestant seminary, I often remarked that relying on the twofold verses about God and Christ as if they are the singular truth about God means not being inclusive of all that Scripture says. If we take the verses about God, Christ, and the Spirit seriously, we already take the verses about God and Christ seriously.

Outside the New Testament, most Evangelicals and Roman Catholics can agree on the Nicene-Constantinopolitan Creed's statements that the Spirit is the Lord, the giver of Life, who proceeds from the Father. We can agree that he is worshipped and glorified with the Father and the Son, and that he has spoken in the prophets. That is a very small set of statements. Yet we need to go back to biblical study, as we have attempted here, to see what place the Spirit has in conversion, in the giving of special gifts, and in the life of personal virtues and social action so that such things will not continue to keep us so far apart that we will not be within hearing distance. At the same time we will need to remember that the divine Spirit blows where the Spirit wills, not waiting for us to agree. And where the Holy Spirit is moving, we should be spiritedly involved.

7. J.N.D. Kelly, *Early Christian Creeds,* 3rd ed. (London: Longmans, 1972) 22–23.

# 7

# The Church:
# One, Holy, Catholic, and Apostolic

Perhaps the best known phrase from the Nicene-Constantino-politan Creed is its description of the Church as "one, holy, catholic, and apostolic." And as we have noticed previously those are words which an overwhelming number of conservative Protestants and Roman Catholics would accept. The reason again rests on a rather simple foundation: both Scripture and Tradition strongly affirm these aspects of the Church.

Yet both conservative Protestants and Roman Catholics are marked by Western concerns. We tend to be consumed by questions of authority and organization and thus find ourselves focused on those queries where we have the most disagreement. Fundamentalists or Evangelicals are expected to see final authority resting in God, but for them authority effectively functions through the Bible and its interpreters. Catholics also confess that final authority rests in God, but effectively their authority functions through Scripture and tradition as interpreted by the magisterium. Again in terms of expectations, conservative Protestants offer a series of organizational patterns, all the way from autonomous local congregations to presbyteries and synods of national and international scope. Roman Catholics find their organizations focused in bishops, councils and particularly in the papacy. These expectations are seldom unfulfilled and thus disagreements between these groups can be regularly predicted.

The Nicene-Constantinopolitan Creed, which is both ecumenical and Eastern, gives us guidance in two important ways. First, it puts the doctrine of the Church under the doctrine of the Holy Spirit and thus within the realm of Trinitarian thought. Talk about the Church comes in the third article which begins with concerns about the Holy Spirit. Thus our Western interests in practical authority and organization as the primary issues which determine the nature of the Church should be challenged by the structure of this creed as well as the Bible itself. When it is so clear that we share a large measure of agreement on the Trinity, why is it that we allow questions of authority to deepen the fissures which separate us? Why is it that both Protestants and Catholics allow the doctrine of the Holy Spirit to be the least understood of the features of the Trinity, and thus weaken any attempts to view the Church primarily under the rubrics of the Spirit and the Trinity? I have no good answers for those questions, but I suspect that were we to return to the guidance of the Nicene-Constantinopolitan Creed we might find a fresh sense of our similarity and a forceful perspective on our differences.

Second, the creed offers us no information whatsoever about proper or improper Church organization. The canons of the Council of Constantinople, and certainly the council itself with its bishops, worked from a specific sense of proper organization. That stands without question. But you could be a Christian who accepts the guidance of the Nicene-Constantinopolitan Creed and recognizes its silence about organization. You could confess the apostolic faith and be unsure about which organizational scheme is best for the Church in a particular age. Russian Orthodox thinkers as well as some conservative Protestants confess that the *consensus fidelium* which we seek is formed not merely by the appointed bishops, but by a much larger group of believing Christians. In the 1930s Sergius Bulgakov rather pointedly responded to a metropolitan who condemned his teaching that he would not accept such a judgment until it was clear that it represented the *sobornost,* "the common mind," of the Church, not merely the opinion of a particular Church official. There had been no general discussion of his views within the wider Church.[1] Indeed Bul-

---

1. William Robinson, the best theologian of my tradition, in his *Whither Theology* (London, Lutterworth Press, 1947) 23–24, n. 1, quotes an unpublished memorandum from Bulgakov dated October, 1935, from Paris. Vatican II speaks of a *sensus fidei* which the whole body of Christ manifests in "a universal con-

gakov in the 1990s is far better known as a significant Christian leader than metropolitan Sergius who opposed him. Even the Council of Constantinople itself was recognized as an ecumenical council, a universal guide, only when more groups of Christians —some official, some unofficial—were willing to take seriously the truth contained in its creed. Schemes of organization do not determine the nature of the Church. They do not indicate whether you or I may recognize another person or group as part of the Christian family. We would be well-advised to heed that silent reminder from the creed, because neither the New Testament nor the history of the Church provides one clear organizational structure for the Church.

In spite of what appears on the surface to be a series of major difficulties, the Church is one, holy, catholic and apostolic. The oneness of the Church has continuously fallen on the rocks of division. I have never met a Christian who did not in some way have a sense of anguish about such divisions. At ecumenical gatherings I have seen the tears flow as those who participated were wounded once more by the clear sense that we as Christians are not one. Yet on the other side I have been overcome by joy at the amount of unity we can share. At the recent dedication of St. Mary's Church during the Thanksgiving season in my home town of Johnson City, Tennessee, people from local Christian Churches, Methodist Churches, Presbyterian Churches and probably others unknown to me worshipped together in an atmosphere of celebration. I prayed a prayer of thanksgiving for all the Roman Catholic Church has done to keep the faith and led a litany I selected which included thanks for the compassion of John Paul II. I do not agree with everything he has said or all that Roman Catholicism has been in its history. But I choose to emphasize the ways in which we can be thankful for each other and to express the needs we have for each other.

The prayer of our Lord in John 17 was that we be one and live out our unity both within and for the world. Yet there are times when a kind of common sense tells us that diversity represents

sent in matters of faith and morals." But it is the magisterium which guides the people of God and which is to be obeyed. *Vatican II: The Conciliar and Post Conciliar Documents,* ed. Austin Flannery, O.P., New Rev. Ed. (Northport, N.Y.: Costello Publishing Company, 1984) 28. *Lumen gentium* 12, 363.

a strength rather than a weakness. A number of ecclesiastical and scholarly pragmatists have argued, often both cogently and persuasively, that the various denominations serve a useful purpose since there exists no possibility of full, bodily union among us. These people are not unaware of the dangers represented by hardened divisions, but they also recognize the truth of a fully fractured humanity, one which like Humpty Dumpty cannot in any real world be put back together again. Such opinions come not only from contemporary leaders who have struggled to agree on some essentials of unity and those who recognize the variances firmly rooted in different human cultures; they also come from careful students of earliest Christianity who remind us that all the information we have from the New Testament and the patristic period indicates how often disagreement and division reigned.

The previously standard views of a Tertullian or a Eusebius have been punctured beyond repair. Heresy was not always later and smaller than orthodoxy. The work of Walter Bauer has been overrated; he has not made his case that in nearly every instance known to us outside of Rome so-called heresy was earlier and larger than orthodoxy. He far too often read evidence with a quirky sense of short phrases and at times just did not carefully consider the texts at hand. But he has left all of us in his debt in that we now recognize our situation in contemporary Christendom as having more similarity to the earlier periods of Christianity than we had formerly assumed.[2]

This applies to the New Testament as well. The unevenness of its tenets must be given their due; historical-critical study of the documents does not allow them to be homogenized or run through a blender. Rough edges remain. Jesus' immediate disciples probably give us all a sense of hope for salvation, not because they are immovable rocks of consistency and courage, but because formerly confused and unfaithful, self-serving and dense, they found their way. James and John could ask for the best seats in Christ's coming kingdom (Mark 10:3-45). Another text has their mother make the request (Matthew 20:20-28). Peter and Paul violently disagreed about whether Jews and Gentiles should eat together and thus break the food laws. They argued at Antioch (Galatians

---

2. Walter Bauer, *Orthodoxy and Heresy in Earliest Christiantiy,* trans. by a team, ed. Robert A. Kraft and Gerhard Krodel (Philadelphia: Fortress Press, 1971).

2:11-21). The Epistle called 2 Peter finds some parts of Paul's epistles difficult to understand (3:15-16). Paul's Galatians and the epistle of James—which James we do not know—may not be contradictory, but at the least their emphases differ considerably.

This tale continues well through the patristic period, the only other period, outside that of the Bible, which we share fully as Protestants and Catholics. Tertullian, who fashioned much of the Trinitarian and Christological language of the Latin West— perhaps with considerable assistance from old Latin translations not fully available to us—offered his contributions to those who lived around the Mediterranean, but he eventually became a Montanist, a "charismatic" if you will, who vigorously fought against the Church developing around him. Although Cyprian and Augustine made great contributions to Western Christianity, particularly in the doctrine of the Church, both failed to root Christianity in North Africa among the native populations of the region. W.H.C. Frend has demonstrated that Donatism came from social and cultural roots basically unaddressed by the great Latin theologians.[3] Furthermore Latin theologians often had little knowledge of their Greek counterparts. And the Greek-speaking theologians were often condescending about their Latin-speaking contemporaries. Gregory Nazianzen ridiculed such teachers. For him it would be impossible to build a Latin theology since the language itself was such a rudimentary, unsophisticated mangle. Even Augustine partially agreed.[4]

The East offers no solace for those who would find a concrete oneness of the Church in this earlier era. The Eastern Orthodox eventually declared their most original thinker, Origen of Alexandria, the single intellectual light comparable to Augustine in the West, a flaming heretic. Yet Origen fed much Western monastic piety through his Scripture commentaries and a school of modern French Catholics has questioned his standing as a heretic with remarkable force. The struggle of the East from the third through the sixth century with Origen and other figures well shows the

3. W.H.C. Frend, *The Donatist Church: A Movement of Protest in Roman North Africa* (Oxford: Clarendon Press, 1952). Frend is a previous holder of the Tuohy chair at John Carroll University.

4. Gregory Nazianzen *Or* 21:35. Augustine, *On the Trinity* 5:8-9; 7:4, noticed the difficulty a Latin speaker had with the Greek used for the Trinity.

disagreements which marked the Eastern Church during the period. Even the Council of Constantinople, like its predecessor among ecumenical councils, the one at Nicaea, came together to include and to exclude. Neo-Arians and Pneumatomachians, the first noted for questioning the full divinity of Christ, and the second known for denying the divinity of the Spirit, considered themselves to be Christians. They were not philosophical schools of impractical academics who did not worship or live the faith. They had arrogant, educated leaders, but their churches were filled with well-meaning people who worshipped God and tried to live moral lives.

The recognition that our problems of expressing the oneness of the Church are not completely different from Christians during the New Testament or patristic eras may not at first glance be encouraging, but at least it does clear the land of some deeply rooted trees which need to be felled and burned. A forest of misconceptions darkens the landscape, particularly among Fundamentalists, but also among Protestant Evangelicals, Roman Catholics and Eastern Orthodox believers. The tallest of these trees stands for the oneness of the "Church" as long as everybody understands that my tradition, my congregation is the one true "Church." Cyprian declared that there was no salvation outside the Church, by which he meant the Church represented by *his* councils, *his* bishops, *his* congregations. For years Roman Catholicism has had strong and influential representatives who have insisted that there is no salvation at all outside Roman Catholicism. Although there have been equally convinced representatives who have thought otherwise in earlier eras, perhaps the greatest achievement of Vatican II has been the weakening of that exclusive Roman sense of the Church's oneness. Some Roman Catholics now feel free to say that Christians other than Roman Catholics may be saved. At the recent dedication of St. Mary's in my home town, the local priest insisted that no one Church could hold all Christians because there is too much grain to fit in any one bin. I have no doubt that he thinks the best bin is the Roman one. Indeed from conversations with him I know that this priest does not sacrifice his sense of truth in Catholicism, but he is thrilled to be able to recognize Christians among other congregations. The truths of Vatican II are now appearing in discussions at the local level as well as among high-level ecumenical discussions. We must recognize our oneness in the midst of our diversity.[5]

There is little within Fundamentalism or among all Protestant Evangelicals which can have the impact of a Vatican II. Fundamentalists most probably will consider only their kind as assured of salvation. From much of their talk you can tell that such views make all others different kinds of pagan. Thus it is quite easy to rebuke and savage, if only by word. All Christian inquisitions known to me have had at their center a sense of the need to save the opponent. If only Savonarola will recant, if only Servetus will return to a right understanding of faith, he will be saved. We do these inquisitors an injustice when we view them as the lovers of gore and violence. Our modern pictures of them are not well-nuanced. If we had understood their pounding motive of saving the other from the fires of hell, we would be better prepared for the savagery—in word—of some Fundamentalists. When they see God as on their side, all means are appropriate to the end. Such fanatics have often existed and will not go away in this or any other age.

But surely we can begin to understand, both because of the New Testament and patristic evidence, and our own sense of the relativity of cultures and individual experiences, that the one true Church is illusive and not represented in its fullness by any one tradition. Over the years I have found that rather solid opinion among many believers and more than a few clerics. My own tradition has had segments which have suffered and made others suffer almost immeasurably because of their sense of their own ultimate truthfulness and holiness. Yet again graciously it has also had representatives who never claimed that the oneness of the Church was expressed completely and exclusively in our heritage or in any one of our congregations.

If Christian diversity is factual, if some variations are not ungracious, then there will be those who suggest that we should concede the field to the pragmatists and confess that every person will take his or her own road to Christian salvation whichever denomination that may be. Such a view has its own sense, one

---

5. *Vatican II Documents,* ed. Flannery, New Rev. Ed., 32. *Unitatis redintegratio* 3–4, 455–459.

which is strongly represented among people who have continuous contact with neighbors and others in the community or in the work place who have quite different beliefs. But I doubt that we can claim to represent the Christian heritage if belief in God, Christ, and the Holy Spirit is so described as to support any way of salvation, any path to personal fulfillment. Yet the problems are large. Even as we look at other religions, we must not insist that all truth lies within Christianity. Genesis 14, Psalm 110 and Hebrews 5-7 see Melchizedek as a priest of God although he does not come from Jewish stock. Proverbs 22-24 contain a number of verses which probably were taken from Egyptian wisdom. In Acts 17 Paul and Luke could mention two passages from Hellenistic philosophers as true: "In him we live and move and have our being" and "for we are indeed his offspring." Theologians from the patristic period often chose carefully from non-Christian sources. We hear much about the Hellenization of early Christian doctrine, an old saw with only partial truth. There were instances in which a kind of syncretism obliterated Christian teaching, but they were not as frequent as one might think. Georges Florovsky, a wise Russian Orthodox theologian, often spoke of early Eastern theologians as Christianizers of Hellenism rather than as those who Hellenized Christianity.[6]

Furthermore when we hear about Tertullian asking "What has Athens to do with Jerusalem?" or read about Tatian attacking the foolishness of Greek philosophers, we must remember that both men used a kind of rhetorical logic which they learned from pagan masters, not Christian teachers alone. When we look at other religions or at other systems of values we must expect to find truth as well as falsehood. It will not do for Christian missionaries from any group to assume that the oneness of the Church means all outside their denomination or outside Christianity are distinguishable by their complete error. I do not know how to claim Christian faith and not insist that salvation comes through

6. Georges Florovsky, "Christianity and Civilization," *St. Vladimir's Seminary Quarterly* 1 (1952) 13-20 reprinted in *Christianity and Culture: The Collected Works of Georges Florovsky* (Belmont, Mass.: Nordland Publishing Company, 1974) 121-130. Adolf von Harnack, *History of Dogma,* trans. from the 3rd ed. by Neil Buchanan (New York: Dover Publishers, 1961) saw the Fathers hellenizing Christianity.

Jesus Christ. But both Scripture and Tradition claim that all truth is not within Christianity alone, nor any particular group of Christians who see things alike. If Jesus did not know certain things and Paul at times had doubt or despair, we should not run our lives of faith on an engine of arrogant presumption which is inappropriate for us and a certainty evidently unnecessary for Jesus. As Christians we have little choice but to preach and witness to Christ as Lord; that must be—and can happily be—our watchword, yet we must always remember what a load of humility that must entail.

I know a now middle-aged Chinese woman who resisted Christianity quietly but firmly all during her primary and secondary education in Taiwan among Roman Catholic nuns. They continually reminded her of the pagan character of her nationality and culture. She found them to be ignorant. Where was their Christianity when the great cultural achievements of the Chinese were developed? Her family was incensed but shrewd. They wanted her to have a modern education of Western style. She herself became a Christian only through the witness of a young man who accepted the customs of her family while he visited them and sought to discover the truths found in her heritage. Such humility made sense in the face of Chinese learning. But this young fellow also found the apostolic faith to be imperative. On those two bases she could see the importance of becoming a Christian.

Perhaps as we confess the diversity within Christian faith, a diversity which is at its root, we will be able to accept each other more readily and thus be prepared for the mission of the Church within the wider world. We can hardly come to an appreciation of other religions and value systems if we continue—against the overwhelming evidence—to insist that our specific way of looking at Christianity is the one true way in the sense that there is not a smidgen of truth elsewhere.

It is, however, both proper and intelligent to look for the oneness manifested in the history of the Church. That oneness may be much more difficult to detail than we might have anticipated, but there must be some way to offer characteristics of Christian faith which are generally acceptable. We must again be forewarned that no perfect agreement is possible at the same time that we search for a *consensus fidelium* which will guide us all to the recognition of our identity and our tasks. In these chapters I have been using the Nicene-Constantinopolitan Creed to help define that *consensus*. And like many other standards from the early Church it calls us to a humble recognition that the Church is one. Perhaps we are forced to offer a minimalist definition if we are to be Biblical and Traditional. Those who take Jesus as the Son of God are Christians. They may be our erring brothers and sisters, in fact, infuriating kith and kin, but they are part of the family. Our task is to take such people seriously and talk with them, rather than always going back into our own groups and feeling at home with those of like precious opinions, social status, educational attainments, racial background, or political views.

It is in the midst of this task that the second feature of the Church which the creed specifies can be taken seriously. The Church is holy. It is set apart for a purpose; it is filled with the saints. Yet at the same time we within the churches continue to be poor examples of any conception of holiness. I can remember a rather spirited lecture by a former professor whose thesis was simple: in most places a good bar will offer more support and care than an average congregation. Tragically that can be argued on a case-by-case basis. But each of us must not forget that we are called to be indwelt by Christ or the Spirit of Christ in such a way that our lives portray that Spirit.

We often cheapen our attempts to submit to the Spirit by making the life of Christian virtue into finicking little lists of "Do this and don't do that" which wear out patience and good sense. Piety worn on the sleeve often only destroys blouses and shirts. Jesus, according to upstanding Jewish leaders, appeared in the wrong places with the wrong people doing the wrong things. A young man who became my best friend in the last years of high school was shocked when those in our youth group turned out to be human beings who did not carry pocket testaments everywhere they went and obnoxiously witness on every street corner. He was a loveable sort from a badly splintered home. On more than one Saturday night we would get his drunken dad from the Elks club and carry him to the car. What I remember the most about his father was his weight, a heavy influence indeed. My friend was funny as he learned Scripture. Only he knew the story of Philip and the eunuch as the story of Paul and the unicorn.

But his entrance into Christianity came from the recognition of both a divine something else within the Church and a clear human something recognizable as well.

There is a holiness in the Church, expressed in life and in worship. Having seen a few bars, I don't find them salvific. Of course we Christians can be hypocrites; we do not always mirror Christ. But in worship, in prayer and in service we see something within our gathered and scattered congregations which is better than what we are in ourselves. We will never outrun our reputation for failure nor cease to be those with warts and fangs. In our midst, however, a difference can be experienced which goes beyond our own possibilities and does reflect our Lord and his Spirit. Once again holiness is something which Protestant Evangelicals and Roman Catholics both find necessary in the Church.[7]

Third, the creed calls the Church catholic; it is universal.[8] The Church can exist in any culture and be a part of the worldwide body of Christ. Perhaps we have spent enough time noting our problems of oneness and holiness that we can emphasize our catholicity in spite of its apparent absence. One of our greatest concerns within a discussion of Protestant Evangelicals and Roman Catholics must be the recognition of how this term has been misused by all concerned. Often the word "catholic" is taken to mean Roman Catholic. For some within Roman Catholicism the only way to be "catholic" with a little "c" is to be "Catholic" with a big "C." For them no one can be a worldwide, universal Christian without being a member of the Roman Catholic Church.

Those disinterested in any discussions between Protestant Evangelicals and Roman Catholics reflect such considerations. Johnny Carson has provoked roars of laughter in an absurd situation with

7. Vatican II, in describing the Church, has a chapter on a call to holiness. See *Vatican II Documents,* ed. Flannery, New Rev. Ed., 28. *Lumen gentium* 39–42, 396–402.

8. My own tradition has insisted that a number of its features are catholic: the name "Christian Church," the confession of Jesus as Lord, the practice of adult immersion baptism for remission of sins, the celebration of the Lord's Supper each Lord's day, the use of the Bible as the norm of faith and practice, a polity centered on local leadership by elders and deacons, and a spirit of catholic unity. Yet in the last fifty years the sense of catholicity has weakened as the sense of conservative Protestantism has increased.

the response: "Is the pope Catholic?" To add the proper note to our reflections, I am told there is even a board game called "Is the pope Catholic?" What could be clearer? Yet for many conservative Protestants that is a significant question, not just one laced with humor because of its obviousness. "Is the pope catholic," a catholic with a little c, not the big C? There is no doubt in anyone's mind that the papacy is a central institution of Roman Catholicism. That surely is not the issue. But the question is whether or not the papacy is the universal feature of the Church, one that can lay claim to being of the essence of the Church.

In the attempt to validate that claim, three steps are usually taken. First, Roman Catholics with strong biblical interests sometimes suggest that the exchange between Peter and Jesus in Matthew 16:13-19 shows how Peter is the rock on which the Church is built, how he is the one who controls the keys of the kingdom. Second, the acceptance of a model of progression or growth toward maturity forms a formidable claim. Were any of us first to see an acorn and then be told that it is only the beginning stage of an oak, we would have to have analogies of other seeds or other biological developments to understand the relationship. Those who argue for the papacy as an essential part of the Church usually accept some such model. Third, they often make a very concerted effort to find the papacy present at Rome as early as possible, surely by the end of the second century and push the acorn back as far as the presence of both Peter and Paul in Rome during the apostolic period.

In response to these points the following may be emphasized. First, the history of biblical interpretation does not clearly support the claim that Matthew 16:13-19 set up Peter as the apostle who alone is the rock on which the Church is built and the one who controls the keys to the kingdom. Matthew 18:18 gives all the apostles the power to bind and loose. In context it is precisely Peter who is rebuked as Satan in Matthew 16:22-23 when he impulsively urges Jesus not to go to Jerusalem and die. The poetic play with Peter's name "Rock" and the rock on which the Church stands has puzzled many interpreters within the Roman Catholic heritage. Thomas Aquinas in his *Catena Aurea,* a collection of what the Church fathers have to say about the four gospels, shows quite clearly that these fathers did not all make the papacy the rock on which the Church stood. John Chrysostom made the confession of Jesus as the Christ the foundation rock and Peter's understanding that of a shepherd. Cyril of Alexandria emphasized that the keys of the kingdom were exercised by many bishops. Even Augustine noted in his *Retractions* that although he had often claimed Peter himself was the rock, now in correcting his views, he saw that the rock was Christ. The careful reader should choose. Origen of Alexandria, somewhat suspect as an orthodox thinker, is quoted by Aquinas as saying that everyone can be a rock who imitates Peter. Rabanus Maurus said that Peter was given a special place for the sake of unity, but the power of the keys was given to the other disciples and thus to bishops and presbyters in every church. And Jerome warned that those using the keys should not be pretentious like the Pharisees. They should recognize that they only know the difference between leprosy and health; they do not heal, for God does that. There is a gloss, perhaps from Aquinas himself, that states the importance of having one principal vicar in Christianity, but Aquinas knows that important Roman Catholic thinkers did not see these Matthew passages as universally supportive of a papal office over all others.[9]

Second, the style of argumentation which plays with the picture of the acorn and the oak has merit. We often see such growth in various organisms, a type which leads to dominant features appearing only at later stages. Indeed, a significant problem in the questions surrounding abortion is that a fetus just a few weeks old does not look human even though the twenty-four week fetus clearly is. But argument on the basis of such models must somehow make rather close connections between the earliest stages and the later developments or the argument is quite weak, perhaps even a failure. Is there an indication that the pope must be the vicar of Christ on earth or the Church will be the headless horseman? Certainly among many conservative Protestant groups there is enough mindless bickering among petty authorities that we can wonder about the headless horseman of Halloween terror. But in terms of what we know about the earliest Church,

---

9. Thomas Aquinas, *Catena Aurea: Commentary on the Four Gospels Collected out of the Works of the Fathers,* trans. Mark Pattison (Oxford: John Henry Parker, 1841), St. Matthew, Vol. I, Part II, 579–592.

Christianity was possible and proper without the papacy. Looking from outside Roman Catholicism as a conservative Protestant, I am not convinced that people must accept the papacy in order to be a Christian, and thus to be catholic, small "c," Christians.

Third, the universality of a unified papacy is not historically demonstrable for all periods of Christianity although Roman Catholicism clearly teaches that the papacy does provide the point of Christian unity.[10] The papal claim was itself not there at the earliest periods of Roman Christianity. When Victor, bishop of Rome about 180 C.E., insisted that Easter should be celebrated only as the Roman Church celebrated it, the knowledge of Tradition, pastoral concern and a deep sense of the unity rather than the uniformity of the Church brought letters from both Polycrates and Irenaeus in favor of an Eastern, non-Roman dating. The decision of the Roman bishop was not seen as unquestionable. As I noted earlier Roman bishops did not accept the Nicene-Constantinopolitan Creed at first, but they eventually were of a different mind. Some careful historians find the strongest proponents of papal infallibility appearing in periods when the Church was under strong attack from outside and weakened from struggles within. That is particularly true of the situation surrounding Vatican I when that teaching was declared a doctrine of the Church. Again it is difficult to know if the nature of the Church is best described for all ages in the midst of times when it is so besieged. Certainly those decades have a place in any description of catholicity, and thus must not be moved aside. But what other phenomenon would you want to describe primarily in terms of its mechanism for defense against the most destructive elements: a bear in hibernation, a cornered tiger, a frog buried in the mud? Those examples are not meant to be fair representations of all aspects of the papacy. But they do point up the problems which Roman Catholic historians and theologians face in responding to the declaration of papal infallibility. Protestant Evangelicals tend to argue that the earliest Church was present in its fullness during the New Testament period and did not wait for further developments to become the oak.

10. See particularly *Vatican II Documents,* ed. Flannery, New Rev. Ed., 28. *Lumen gentium* 22, 25, 374–376, 379–381.

I would also be remiss if I did not point out the stark parallelism between Roman Catholic claims of papal infallibility and Fundamentalist and Evangelical claims of biblical inerrancy. In each case a kind of logic is involved which sets up definitions that cannot be affected by facts. The meetings of Evangelicals in Chicago during 1978 and 1986 warned that a definition of biblical inerrancy should not be weakened by what the Bible actually says in places where it was not defining its own authority. That kind of argumentation boggles the mind. What the Bible says cannot be used to define what the Bible is, except in those few passages where the Bible is said to be giving a definition of itself. For me, the whole Bible, read from cover to cover, will determine what it is, not just selected verses. Those evangelical conferences also insisted that no modern sense of exact science should be used in working with Scripture. We should expect that not all the dates will fit, not all the "science" will be like our science today. I pointed out in the second chapter that this was death by a thousand qualifications.

The same holds true for a definition of papal infallibility. Such definitions have to dance a bit, to squirm a little, if they take seriously the history of the papacy. One of the problems with theologians is that we often use words in strange ways. The more we talk about God, who surpasses all definitions, the less alarmed we should be when that talk seems different. But when we move on into the more human endeavors where people are an imposing part of writing Scripture, or where persons occupy the place of pope, it is difficult not to be more interested in the history. In the seventeenth century Protestants reacted to the resurgence of Catholicism with a definition of biblical inerrancy. In the nineteenth century Catholicism reacted to the growth of secular forces with a definition of papal infallibility. Neither definition seems adequate for two reasons at least. First, they both do not fit the information they attempt to explain. Second, they both are negatives and need few facts to destroy their sense.

This is where the most difficulties arise between the two groups. Yet it is also where I find them both the most wanting. The Western penchant for authority, the search for where the buck stops, has taken a toll on both these heritages. Protestant Fundamentalists still insist that biblical inerrancy—sometimes referred to as biblical infallibility—must be defended or the clear sense of revelation will be lost. That is most often joined with a sense of propositional revelation and logic which defies common human speech and pays too little attention to inductive arguments and thus to history. Roman Catholicism is in some ways no better. The doctrine of papal infallibility was expressed officially in a period when Christianity was not doing well in its struggle with Western culture. To me the function of the doctrine was to set up an immovable rock upon which the life of faith could be built. But the definition of the doctrine and its historical context make it clear that it is difficult to defend either theologically or historically, particularly in the latter arena.

These two doctrines are in many ways what most separate conservative Protestants and Roman Catholics, and they each represent the most suspect position taken by each group. I do not imagine that these doctrines will disappear quickly, but I cannot help but express my sadness that these weakest points are so divisive. Yet Scripture does tell us that the gates of hell shall not prevail against the Church and the history of the Church shows how stubbornly it has hung on in difficult times. There is a positive sense from Scripture and Tradition that God will lead his Church, that God will not allow it to die and will empower it to overcome error. Perhaps if we Protestant Evangelicals and Roman Catholics were less concerned about ordination and office, less interested in lines of authority and seats of power, we could rest in the promise that the plans of God will not be thwarted, no matter how difficult it may appear to us in any particular age.

I have a mixed sense of various popes. I was not alive when the concordats made with Mussolini allowed him to invade Ethiopia, but I do not find those decisions defensible. Yet I have been quite impressed with the work of John XXIII and now with aspects of John Paul II's efforts. As Christian leaders they have had remarkable influence for good, not infallible in my view, but remarkable none the less. I would like to give them their due. The spirit of John XXIII so penetrated the life of worldwide Christianity that when I held an interim ministry at a Church of God some years ago, one of the fine women in that congregation gave me a book the contents of which were meditations of John XXIII. That was an exchange between two conservative Protestants in which the words of a Roman Catholic pope were the gift. I recognize that the influence of a man like John Paul II when he celebrates a Mass among thousands of Poles does much more for good than I can accomplish in my career. While there is always the possibility for evil when so much power is in the hands of one person or a small group like the curia, there is also the possibility of much good. The difference between John Paul II bending to kiss the ground of each country he visits and Tammy Faye Bakker bending to kiss her own driveway has not passed me by.

When we speak of ministry and authority, it is also important to recognize that Protestant Evangelicals, while usually united in their opposition to an infallible papacy, are quite disunited in their sense of how the Church could be organized. Free church bodies like my own are congregationally autonomous; each local church operates as it sees fit. Although there are some shared modes of organization, there are no associations of churches from which a particular congregation can be excluded, such as a synodal system used by Presbyterians or local, state and national associations employed by Baptists. During the rise of contemporary Fundamentalism, my humorous eye has been turned to Church organization. Within some conservative Presbyterian Churches and certainly within the Southern Baptists, there are state and national structures which can be captured if enough delegates can be persuaded to vote in that way. Fundamentalists now control the Southern Baptist machinery although they are not a majority within all the Southern Baptist Churches. In my tradition there is nothing to capture. You can argue that someone else is a liberal, that some institution is unworthy of Christian support. But you cannot storm the citadel, take over the fortress, and put anyone out.

Of course at a local level you could capture the board and change the direction of the local congregation. That has been done. And you can be a participant in some remarkable meetings of local boards, ones in which personality quirks tend to be a major influence on the decisions, sometimes for good or ill, sometimes just for the craziness of it all. One of my grandfather's favorite stories concerned a man in the church who was, as my grandfather put it, "born in the objective case." He always looked gloomy and was at best a crusty person, yet he had enough virtues to have been on the board for years; no one wished to remove him. At one board meeting, he came up with a brilliant idea. The rest of the board was stunned at the progressive, enlightened insight. Someone quickly seconded the idea and put the question to a vote. When the roll was called, the old curmudgeon was the last on the list. Reckoning that if all the rest of them thought his idea was good, it must be bad, he voted against his own motion. You do not avoid the oddity of humanity when in a free church you have no regional, state, or national structure. Structures can be workable in some instances, unworkable in others. In any case they do not represent the nature of the Church, only its outworkings in various cultural situations.

The catholicity of the Church is most probably not rooted in its organization. Vincent of Lérins described it as what has been taught and believed everywhere by everyone. That would have to be a minimalist conception, a difficult one to defend. But even within an apparently American frontier tradition like my own, with all its individualism and provincialism, one of our early leaders, Alexander Campbell, more than once insisted that the New Testament should be the norm of faith and practice, but also that nothing should be required for the unity of the Church except those aspects of faith and practice that are universally recognized by all Christians. That is why the most significant description of our churches is free-church catholic. Yet we have failed in many ways to embody that kind of catholicity. It is no mean feat, one that can only be received as a gift from God, not reached as an achievement. Yet it is important that we continue to talk together, we conservative Protestants and Roman Catholics, so that we can be the Church catholic. To do so we will have to be in contact with more traditions than the Roman or Protestant ones. But that is a tale for another time.

Fourth, the Church is apostolic. The clearest mark of apostolicity is the New Testament itself. Conservative Protestants and Roman Catholics share Scripture together. The New Testament has both been a norm of faith and practice as well as a launching pad for remarkable speculative flights among Evangelicals and Catholics. Roman Catholics have had periods of deep biblical renewal. In fact it is the Tradition of the Church that has declared Scripture to be the touchstone of Christian faith, for many the norm of faith and practice. Today a number of Protestant Evangelicals are beginning to see the faithful function of Tradition in the life of the Church. If my observations are correct such is a mark of the present era. It is possible to be a pious Roman Catholic and humbly suggest that faith be seen primarily in what Scripture entails. Catholics of such persuasion were vocal both at the Council of Trent and at Vatican II. Protestant Fundamentalists and Evangelicals have followed the lead of the sixteenth-century Reformation and argued sharply for *sola scriptura*. But some contemporary Evangelicals have begun to give a proper place to Tradition and catholic substance. Some are working their way through the maze of traditional systematic theologies toward more biblical frameworks for their own thought. For the Church to be the Church it must be apostolic, it must bear the mark of the apostles. That is a part of its oneness, its holiness and its catholicity. Instead of being constantly alert to the ordering of these aspects in a kind of chicken-egg argument, we would do well to remember that apostolicity was indeed an historically early mark of the Church, but that apostolicity was part of the catholic consensus which gave us the canon.

Any Roman Catholic must recognize that the significance of Scripture is a catholic—little "c"—a universal position. Any Protestant should concede that the Great Church recognized and preserved our Scripture. Here we can offer no either/or solutions, because there are none. Too few Fundamentalists are concerned with mutual relations with Roman Catholics outside of saving Catholics from their sins. Yet even in those circles there is a grudging respect for Roman Catholicism's resistance to the dreaded Liberalism. Among Protestant Evangelicals that same respect has been enlarged by a vision shared on a much wider scale. Both Evangelicals and Catholics have made valiant, if not always successful, attempts to understand and incorporate historical-critical study of Scripture within their approaches to faith. They have often been conservative, not convinced that reductionistic world views can do full justice to Scripture. And in ways which are as yet not well-recognized, many Evangelicals have found a creative and helpful place for the Church and Tradition in their understanding of faith. The old saw of Bible versus Church is not heard as often as previously.

The Church is one, holy, catholic and apostolic. When it is not, it weakens its own nature, attacks its own life as cancer consumes healthy cells. It may appear bothersome to think of Evangelical Protestants and Romans Catholics needing each other in order for the Church to be herself, but it is unavoidable. And once you grasp that, you are in for some of the most uplifting experiences of your Christian life. You will know pain, but you will also know more about God, Christ and the Spirit who give us all life.

# 8

# Christian Worship and Life

The Nicene-Constantinopolitan Creed does not speak explicitly of worship or the ethical life but as a confession its setting is intended to be a service of worship. Indeed its final phrases, its concern for baptism and forgiveness as well as the resurrection and life everlasting, form the context in which worship and life are expressed. Baptism for the remission of sins creates a different relationship between not only the believer and God but also that believer and other believers. The Apostles' Creed speaks of the communion of saints and thus poetically emphasizes both the sacramental character of baptism and the Eucharist as well as the communion of the present-day faithful with those who have gone on to their reward.[1] The parallel between the resurrection of Jesus Christ and the resurrection of the believer is often a motif within worship. And the sense of Christ's second coming and the gift of eternal life have engendered deep effects on how Christians live their lives. Hell-fire and damnation sermons have been a staple of conservative Protestant revivals, but warnings from nuns or priests about coming judgment and its possible horrors have

1. See Berard L. Marthaler, *The Creed* (Mystic, Conn.: Twenty-Third Publications, 1987) 347–368 who points out this double sense of the *communion sanctorum*. Ch. 4 of *Lumen gentium,* the document on the Church from Vatican II, deals with the "Pilgrim Church." Within that chapter is not only a clarification of the cult of the saints but also a stirring presentation of the communion with the saints who have gone on before us. See *Vatican Council II: The Conciliar and Post Conciliar Documents,* ed. Austin Flannery, O.P., New Rev. Ed. (Northport, N.Y.: Costello Publishing Company, 1984) vol. 1, 28, 48–51, 407–413.

not been absent from Roman Catholic education and liturgy. Yet as for the Apostle Paul, the almost inexpressible value of baptism, Eucharist, resurrection and eternal life with God and the saints is the overwhelming positive emphasis: worship as celebration and life as loving response. Indeed it would be difficult to describe the fundamental structure of Christian worship and life without reference to these last phrases of the creed. The negative aspects of sacraments and eschatology, however, must not be ignored; it has taken both carrot and stick to move many a jackass. Thus some sense of the context of worship and life which Roman Catholics and conservative Protestants share must be explored if we are to see the characteristics of catholic Christianity in ourselves and others. And these phrases from the creed confess truths that once again most conservative Protestants and Roman Catholics do share.

Many candid observers, however, find the relationship of worship and life between the two groups ambiguous. Whenever I am given the opportunity, I make it a point to worship in an atmosphere different from that provided by my own heritage. The differences are so clear that at first I feel alien even though I have had some practice on two continents in two languages. When my wife and I were first learning to hear and speak German by attending a language school in Salzburg, Austria, we attended services in the Roman Catholic cathedral there because we thought our sense of Christian worship and life would help us understand. That proved to be true. We will never forget how we could participate in a Christian celebration within a foreign country on the basis of another language because we knew enough of Christian speech to anticipate what was involved. That the congregation was a Roman Catholic one, that it was where we could find enough similarities with our previous Christian experience to learn the new language was not a point lost on us. Yet the experience itself was both religiously and culturally marked by being not merely similar but also different, even odd at points. To sit in a Roman Catholic service presented in the English language takes a bit of work on my part. I do not know the liturgy as well as regular worshippers and must pay close attention to notes in the printed order and to the pages in the service book. What should I repeat? When do I stand? Do I kneel at any particular point?

Should I take the wine and the bread? At times the hymns in the books have no music with them. I can read music, but how do I sing an unprinted melody I do not know? Furthermore, at times those actively involved in the service are dressed in a garb which is not used by the leaders of my congregation. They process through the service carrying utensils equally foreign to my experience. A first-time attender who is a conservative Protestant might ask: Are these people putting on a play; are they playing church? What is the point?

There is a grand point. The Church is older than the United States. As I said once to one surprised teenager, it is even older than your grandmother. It has traditions which come from lands we seldom think about, let alone know anything about. The large church organizational structures, the liturgies, the vestments, all try to remind us that no early American invented the faith. The beauty of many liturgies is in their poetry, their cadences, their incorporation of Scripture in so many ways that most Roman Catholic Churches on any given Sunday will have more actual Bible verses spoken or read in their services than would be a part of the service in an average conservative Protestant congregation. Some Protestant Evangelicals are high church Anglicans or Lutherans, perhaps well-traditioned Presbyterians or Methodists who have developed liturgical customs and expertise.[2] They know the tradition. But many evangelical Protestant churches need more attention to liturgy, need to know what a lectionary is. That cycle of biblical passages set up to lead a congregation through most if not all of Scripture in a specified period is true both to Scripture and to Tradition. Furthermore most conservative Protestants need to understand the importance of the eye as well as the ear in worship, an insight particularly important in our television era.

But there are also weaknesses in most Roman Catholic churches. So many Roman Catholic priests have been taught to concentrate on the liturgy that they often are not particularly good preachers. Some homilies are neither scintillating nor helpful. During my course at John Carroll University about televangelists, a few students made the comment that they wished their priests

---

2. For a description of why some have moved toward such experiences see Robert E. Webber, *Evangelicals on the Canterbury Trail: Why Evangelicals Are Attracted to the Liturgical Church* (Waco, Tex.: Jerrell, 1985).

could make the gospel as interesting as some of the televangelists do. That is a sad comment because a number of the televangelists preach poorly even though they all preach with enthusiasm. Yet Roman Catholic priests could gain from evangelical Protestants both skills for and tradition about preaching. I suspect they could learn a great deal from their own Dominicans who are often remarkable preachers.

As a rule congregational singing among Evangelicals is better than that in Roman Catholic parishes. The gap is lessening but we have had more practice and in fact sing types of hymns which were written for group singing. As you remember, Luther's "A Mighty Fortress is Our God" is set to an old drinking song, one which many people could let rip when it had its former words. The devil need not have all the tunes. That does not mean, however, that there are no oddities within the singing of evangelical churches. Some of the great revivalist hymns of the nineteenth and twentieth centuries have rather good melodies, but words which are fatal. Yet the figure of being washed in the blood or the emphasis on the power in Christ's blood, which have been viewed by some "enlightened" Protestants as so gory that they cross over into bad taste, are perhaps more in line with the piety behind moving depictions on Roman Catholic crucifixes of our dying Lord.

Often it is the sentimental individualism of Protestant revivalist hymns which is most disturbing, the claim that Jesus and I have shared close experiences which "none other has ever known," not exactly what you would see as an expansive sense of community or Church. There are fundamentalist or evangelical hymns, some taken from experiences among the poor and oppressed, which suggest a piety you might not share. The first time I heard a hymn entitled "The Big Eye in the Sky is Watching You" I did not think of a compassionate Father. Others are striking once you get over the initial shock of the words. The old spiritual, "There ain't no flies on Jesus," sounds bizarre, but it was very effective among those who had watched their loved ones suffer rigor mortis and the beginning of decay without any aid from funeral parlors.

I have also attended conservative Protestant services in which much work had been done on the sermon, but almost none on the liturgy. The plan was simple. The preacher would prepare the sermon, then ask someone to pick a few hymns. Someone else would be asked to pray; others were selected to prepare the communion and pass out the emblems. That was the service. Often evangelical congregations with members who are well-educated and wealthy will demand better buildings and more elaborate and beautiful liturgies. Within my tradition a congregation in Phoenix, Arizona, has a Frank Lloyd Wright building and one of the finest pipe organs in the western United States. It also prepares and organizes its services with much care.

But the general point still stands. Conservative Protestants can share a long tradition of congregational singing and preaching with Roman Catholics, and Roman Catholics can share their lectionaries and liturgies with conservative Protestants. In many ways we need each other because we each provide the various pieces of the puzzle which end up comprising, not compromising, the Church. Separate we suffer deeply from our weaknesses; aware of each other and working toward more recognition and contact with each other we can learn from the others' strengths.

Underneath this public worship we must find ways to acknowledge and share together different spiritualities which again on the surface seem almost diametrically opposed. Roman Catholics have rosaries, candles, positions of kneeling, the sign of the cross, icons, etc.: all of which allow you to make a rather smooth transition from church to home worship. These aids can be handled crassly or thoughtlessly but they can also be material helps for concentrating on what God has done. For some of the more devout, pilgrimages, retreats and other types of assistance in focusing oneself on the central things of the Christian life have become appreciated modes of worship.

Most Protestantism has been accused of having no spirituality, no atmosphere of worship in which the life of virtue has grown out of humble contrition in the presence of God. At times it is difficult if not impossible to discover what deep wells of the Spirit are quenching the thirst of a battling Fundamentalist. But my own experience of the Christian faith has always been founded on an attempt to practice the presence of God. Many conservative Protestants begin each day with some period of prayer, perhaps a few verses of Scripture and a small meditation read at the breakfast table. Clearly the pressures of modern life—get off to work, get the children off to school—have made these times less frequent if they have not obliterated them altogether. But a kind of conservative Protestant piety which knows the freedom of praying without ceasing, of thinking about people and situations and giving them over to God, is not to be rebuked because it has so few material aids. Many of these Protestants pray over their meals no matter where they are. The more devout among them tend to be in church services at least three times a week and perhaps a Bible study/prayer meeting in their own home a fourth time. Yet some Roman Catholics who might attend public worship at one of these services would be struck by how drab and how informal the time together is, how difficult it can be for them to feel the deep movement of the Spirit in this kind of setting.

I have had my own kinds of difficulties in these Protestant services. Even as a small child, right after my baptism at the early age of seven, I knew that the Lord's Supper was something remarkable. I did not want to take the bread and the wine in the same way that I ate other food, so I developed a pattern that I have continued now over forty years. Although I am right-handed I always take those emblems with my left hand so that something is different about this meal from any other that I eat. That doubtless is another quirk of my own personality but it has served me well as a reminder of the difference.

What I have observed every time that I have been in a Roman Catholic Mass is that those participating are practicing a kind of humility in the presence of Christ that makes this part of their lives different. Having grown up around Italian and Irish Catholics I know the way in which their attitudes changed in the presence of the Body and Blood of Christ. Young people who were rough-and-tumble became quiet and meditative; adults whose lives were marked by an earthiness and pleasure in living that tends to match my Midwestern or Southern love of being alive became still and moved into another world. Brash academic friends whose pride in their achievements is merited but who think too highly of themselves become more humane within the Mass.

The best of my own tradition is rather high church, concerned with reverence and a weekly celebration of the Lord's Supper. But as a rule we do not provide quite the deep and broad liturgical sense that a Roman Mass offers. I have more than once indicated, in what we call a communion meditation (a brief talk just before the bread and wine are distributed) that our focus on remembrance is not enough to do justice to the New Testament texts. They claim that these elements are the Body and Blood of Christ. I do not know *how* they are, but I accept the description *that* they are his Body and Blood. Roman Catholic and Eastern Orthodox friends have strengthened that understanding in me although I find it in Scripture itself.

At the same time I must confess that conservative Protestant celebration of the Lord's Supper, often influenced by symbolic interpretations, too often does not create the sense of God's presence as the Mass has done. This is one of those places where as a conservative Protestant, even as a free church catholic, I can only speak of my longing for what the Mass so often provides rather than any criticism of this aspect of it. I feel the need of such structures of reverence and try to introduce some of them into my own congregation and into the lives of the students who come to my classes for instruction.

We must find ways to share our worship and our spirituality so that we can see each other as Christians. We can put up with widely varied aspects of our total lives, but we cannot afford to exclude each other from humble worship of God. We need each other, but real differences bar the way. Many conservative Protestants take seriously the promise of Christ that where two or three are gathered together, there he will be. Some of them prefer to have ordained ministry leading even that small a gathering, but others are not certain that worship can only be valid if its leadership is ordained. That does not mean that their efforts are marked by total disorder or that they seek totally uneducated pastors. Often they see baptism as the necessary ordination for ministry and thus confess a priesthood of all believers. Within traditions that practice adult baptism that connection is stronger and more clearly understood.

We will not agree quickly about such matters; but they must be faced squarely. Vatican II has opened the way for Roman Catholics to look upon those from other communions as Christian sisters and brothers. The participation of a number of conservative Protestants in ecumenical endeavors, much more frequently now than even thirty years ago, has lessened their attacks on Catholics as non-Christians. Earlier in my life when I was less fully aware of the traditional Roman Catholic teaching, I would partake of the wine and the bread when I visited a Roman service where my own beliefs were unknown. Now I no longer do that for I know, both in terms of having had the Roman Mass celebrated as a closed communion within the chapel of my own seminary community and having attended the Mass as a better informed visitor, that those offering the elements would be offended were I to partake. As both a Church historian and a theologian I am aware of the development of the sense of ministry which depends upon apostolic succession. Those views, which appeared in bud no later than the early second century and in flower by the fifth century, suggest that it is improper for the supper of the Lord, the Mass, to be offered to those who are non-Catholics.

One of the great barriers which stands between Christians today is the interpretation of apostolic succession.[3] It is instructive to remember that following in the steps of the apostles has not always meant standing in a line of ordination, an uninterrupted laying on of hands from one to the other. The heritages which see the apostolic character of the Church rooted in "apostolic succession," the unbroken line of ordained priests, have had significant difficulty recognizing the validity of others' ministry. Each heritage can find a gap in the line formed by the others, a slip confirmed by most reasonable historians. A history of the papacy, a history of Anglican bishops, a history of Eastern Orthodox patriarchs, will always find a place in which the line has been interrupted. From a fair perspective, however, it is remarkable that these lines are as firm as they are given the vagaries of history.

Among Protestant Evangelicals there will always be those who do not view apostolicity as defined primarily by apostolic succession.[4] We have seen various agreements or understandings reached

3. Vatican II did not argue the historical case for apostolic succession; it stated it on the basis of Tertullian and Irenaeus as a clear Roman doctrine. *Vatican II Documents,* ed. Flannery, New Rev. Ed., 28. *Lumen gentium* 20, 371-372.

4. See the forthcoming papers of the Consultation on the American-born Churches sponsored by the Faith and Order Group of the National Council of Churches of Christ in the United States, March 13-14, 1991, at the University of Dallas.

among the heritages which rely on the line of bishops in each age. We will probably see more unified opinion in favor of succession, particularly as Lutheran, Anglican and Eastern Orthodox Christians move closer to Roman Catholics. But in my view it is tragic to see ministry which is clearly marked by faithfulness and even recognizable effectiveness condemned as invalid because no proper line of ordination can be established for it.

Both Protestant and Catholic writers who are also troubled about this matter have noted that in various situations where ministry is most needed, such as in prison camps, in isolated regions, and in emergency situations, ministry has occurred without waiting for so-called proper ordination. A good friend of mine retells the story of a faithful Episcopalian family in eighteenth-century southwestern Virginia. Both father and mother struggled to keep their five girls alive in the harsh conditions of subsistence farming. Each fall the father drove some of the hogs to market nearly twenty miles away from the farm so that a bit of cash could be obtained. One year when he was gone on his trip a terrible illness swept through the valley. The poor mother nursed each daughter until that girl died, then dug a grave, buried her, and read the service from the Anglican book of prayer. At the end she had cared for and buried all of their daughters. Who would argue that such ministry would become valid only after it had been brought within the proper "apostolic succession"?

Clerical control of worship and ministry is not new to the history of the Church, but it is not necessarily as definitive as some traditions have insisted. Conservative Protestant traditions are growing in their sense of the need for successive apostolic functions within the Church, activities which must be present where the Church is. Yet some modern theologians who are not conservative Protestants have noted that the Church has been active in places where ordained clergy were either absent or only occasionally present. Jürgen Moltmann was a prisoner of war within a camp near Nottingham, England, where the sacraments were celebrated and ministry functioned, but there were no priests or ministers inside who had been previously ordained.[5] Apostolic ministry was present although formal ordination was not. Leader-

5. Jürgen Moltmann, *Experiences of God,* trans. Margaret Kohl (Philadelphia: Fortress Press, 1980).

ship was present although formal authority was not. The real apostolic succession is Christians meeting the needs of others. We will never recapture the broadest and deepest sense of ministry if we continue to insist on ordination within a clear line of apostolic succession as the key and treat any other attempts to function apostolically in ministry as limited to emergency situations rather than as normal parts of Church life.

Yet Protestant Evangelicals who see the validity of that kind of argument must also confess their own weaknesses in dealing with ministry which is not watched over with a clear sense of mission. There are far too many loose cannons on the evangelical ship. More care in preparing and selecting ministers is in order. It is, however, difficult to know whether congregational, presbyterial, synodal, conciliar, or papal watchfulness of ministry is more effective. We must all be diligent in asking for faithfulness and responsibility from our leaders. In our era the bulk of religious news focuses on the egregious faults of Christian leadership. Some of that is earned. Tragically it makes us edgy and too quickly willing to jettison such problems as belonging primarily to some other denomination, some other suspect group within Christendom. The big play in recent years has been on Fundamentalists like Oral Roberts, Jim Bakker, and Jimmy Swaggert. But during the same period leaders within my own tradition who have been local pastors with no television time were involved in similar escapades. And I am sure that such problems have arisen in situations known to you within your heritage. As always our responsibility is probably not to argue in the midst of these instances for the clear effectiveness of one organizational scheme over another. Rather we need to develop some way to bring together the sense of validity in the pastoral acts, the communal services of these fallen leaders, at the same time that we deplore their sinfulness and call them to repentance and God's forgiveness.

The relationship of ordination and valid ministry will always need our attention but the demands of apostolic succession can also bring deep pain. At a recent meeting of the Faith and Order Working Group of the National Council of Churches of Christ I heard a devoted Roman Catholic woman describe her reaction to a communion service at the Canberra, Australia, meeting of the World Council of Churches. She sat between two priests. None of the three took bread and wine because the celebrant was not validly ordained according to Roman canon law. The first priest went foward and asked for a blessing from one of those offering the emblems. When he returned to his seat, he began to cry and thus joined the woman and the second priest in tears. It is tragic to be separated from each other at the Supper of our Lord.[6]

I can hardly express how sad it makes me to sit in a service with fellow Christians and be barred from participating in the bread and the wine. Were a Roman Catholic to come to Grand-view Christian Church (my congregation) that person would hear public admonishment to look within himself or herself in order to partake of the supper worthily. But no one from our tradition would bar anyone from participating. We grew out of nineteenth-century situations in which only a few could eat and drink the Lord's Supper—those few who held all the proper points of doctrine established by an examination held before the Eucharist was served.

Within conservative Protestantism there is neither any lack of a sense of the apostolic nor any disinterest in apostolic ministry. Often among these groups the New Testament itself defines what is apostolic and what is apostolic ministry. There are leaders who are selected to lead services of communion and to distribute the elements. More than some might expect, there is a special sense of the presence of Christ either within the emblems themselves or within the service.

In response to the age-old problem of poor leadership, many Christians belong to groups, whether Protestant or Catholic, which have highly structured forms of ministry: ensconced and incompetent. We must find ways to admonish, to rebuke, to love, even to rehabilitate leaders who have fallen. Of course, it may be correct to suggest that those who have proved incapable should

6. Vatican II changed many aspects of the official Roman Catholic view of believers outside its ranks, even to the point of calling many of these people "Christians," brothers and sisters in Christ, indicating that such folk can assist in the edification of Catholics, and suggesting that the "Holy Supper" commemorated by such groups has correct features and should become one point of significant dialogue. Yet the council still insists that its Eucharist cannot be celebrated with these "separated churches." See *Vatican II Documents,* ed. Flannery, New Rev. Ed., 32. *Unitatis redintegratio* 3, 8, 22, 455–456, 460–461, 469; 38. *Dans ces derniers temps* 55 (1970) 499 repeats the prohibition.

not again seek leadership positions. Yet in our haste to clean up stinking situations, we need to be careful that we not shovel out the pony which the little boy is certain must be under all that manure. The Church is the body of Christ, one living organism comprised of many members, each of them suited in some way for ministry to the body and to the world. Perhaps in the midst of the difficulty of having fewer and fewer priests, Roman Catholics can recapture the sense that it is the apostolic ministry of the whole body, each part fitted for some special work, that is one of the most important understandings of worship and life. When the Roman Catholic council of bishops here in the United States rejected the possibility of unordained leaders leading funeral services, they lost an opportunity for returning apostolic ministry to the whole Church. However the communion services presided over by lay leaders or women set apart for other ministries, even though they require previously consecrated bread and wine, are a substantial step in a right direction. Married men and women should be able to find their place in leadership when the sacraments are celebrated.

Jesus called people from all walks of life into the kingdom of God. They were not selected because of their gender, their proven skills, or their former creed. For example, the inclusion of women within Christian groups was rather striking in the ancient world, although it did have some analogues within Jewish practice.[7] Jesus depended upon women in his inner circle both for financial support and for the spread of the gospel. Luke 8 tells us of women who gave their money so that Jesus might use his time for other things. According to John 8, Jesus told the Samaritan woman at the well to be the witness in her community, to be the one who proclaimed the gospel to the Samaritans. We know Jesus cared for non-Jews because of that woman and the Syro-Phoenician woman. According to Matthew 15 he apparently baited the latter woman, told her dogs did not eat at the table, but she replied dogs got the crumbs under the table. Jesus declared that her faith was great, thus using this incident to teach his disciples that race and culture are not priorities in his kingdom. As Matthew 28,

---

7. Bernadette Brooten, *Women Leaders in the Ancient Synagogue: Inscriptional Evidence and Background Issues* (Atlanta, Ga.: Scholars Press, 1982) demonstrates the claim of her title: Jewish synagogues did at times have women leaders.

Mark 16, and Luke 24 report, it was women who found the empty tomb and ran to tell the disciples. These females could not give evidence in most if not all Jewish courts. Their report was confirmed by the apostles who ran to the empty tomb, and thus learned not only that Jesus was resurrected but that women were capable witnesses to the most important event of Christian faith.

Paul is the one, however, who in 1 Corinthians 14 seems to tell women to keep quiet in church gatherings, to let their husbands, who are their "heads" within the marriage relationship, explain what has been going on within the service after both of them have returned home. The picture is a relatively simple one. Often within Hellenistic culture, whether pagan or Jewish, women were given a secondary place. When that place was changed within earliest Christianity, when women became full participants in Christian worship, they heard and saw things, were involved in practices, which they had never before witnessed. You can easily imagine Naomi punching Jonathan in the ribs and asking, "What does that mean?" "Why are they doing that?" So Paul merely said that they should not disrupt the service with their questions and later ask those who knew.

The force of that text became clear to me one summer when my family and I were on a retreat with a group of U.S. Army people in Europe. A big enlisted man came knocking at my door after I had given a talk. In his arms he carried a small baby and thus cut quite a pose: tough army man carefully bouncing tiny infant. He had a question which was really bothering him. When he married he was not a Christian; in fact he had just become one in the last few months. He wanted to be a good Christian, a proper husband and father, but he was sorely troubled. He had read 1 Corinthians 14 which said that women should be silent in the church and let their husbands tell them what things meant when they got home. His wife was a teacher, had been a Christian since childhood, and had even taught Sunday School. When he had so many questions about the faith, how could he obey Paul and explain things to his wife who already knew what was going on?

The answer I gave him was simple. "Be quiet and listen in the service, then ask your wife about things when you get home." I don't think I subverted Paul's message; I merely made knowledge and ignorance the primary categories and thus reversed the gender roles. I have heard that some leaders within my tradition were absolutely incensed that I said such a thing to the soldier because I gave exactly the opposite advice to what Paul said. My response is that I think I gave precisely the same advice that Paul did. The knowledgeable teach the ignorant.

Chapter 21 of the book of Acts tells us of Philip's daughters who were prophetesses. We so often think of prophesying as foretelling the future that we forget it was also a kind of forthtelling, a type of preaching that was highly regarded within the earliest Church. Women could preach and did. They were accepted leaders in some Christian circles, accepted in ways that were unusual within the larger culture. When we look at all the evidence about women that can be assembled from the New Testament, it is a rather remarkable collage for documents that come from first century Jewish and Hellenistic culture.

In teaching an introduction to Christian doctrine I am always struck by how, throughout the history of the Church, systematic theology has been dominated by men. Yet if we think of worship as the context of theology and try to find the best writings on Christian spirituality or devotion, women are often the dominant figures. No one would attempt to cover spirituality and leave out the study of Catherine of Siena, Teresa of Avila and many others. Women are strongly represented if we see Christian martyrs and mystics as theologians.

Within both conservative Protestant and Roman Catholic traditions the place of women within the Church is now under discussion, debate, or even on the verge of becoming a debacle. This is one area in which many Evangelicals and Catholics tend to agree on a solution which I find unwarranted by both biblical and traditional sources. Many conservative Protestants, both Fundamentalists and Evangelicals, and a number of Roman Catholics insist that women should not hold the highest positions of leadership in the Church even at the local level. In a recent papal letter concerning the dignity and vocation of women, John Paul II has offered a well-conceived and beautiful tribute to the place of women. The biblical use of feminine language for God is noted. The domination of males and female responsibility for the origin of sin is refuted, and the importance of women within the Old and New Testament communities is emphasized. This is a helpful document that does much to root out any male chauvinism lodged within Christian communities.[8]

Yet the place of women in the Church's ordained ministry is not discussed. What are we to say in that regard about the women who worked within the early circle of Jesus' ministry? Are they somehow much lesser figures, ones incapable of designated ministry? Ungraciously various English translations of Scripture give us strange accounts of specific passages that provide some of the most important information, accounts that support lesser roles for women but do not handle the texts correctly. When Paul speaks of Phoebe in Romans 16 she is often called a "servant" and a "helper" rather than a "deacon" and a "patron." It is odd that the word *diakonos,* which can indeed mean "servant," is in some translations rendered as "deacon" with overtones of authority when it refers to specific men, but as "servant" when it refers to the woman Phoebe. What is behind translations which consistently render a word "servant" for women and "deacon (a position of authority)" for men? John Paul II refers to her as a deaconess.[9]

In that same chapter of Romans "Junia" is sometimes oddly identified as a man, her feminine name said to be a shortened form of the masculine name. In some translations her gender is changed completely by adding the word "men" to the text, when it does not appear there. We know that it is much more likely that the reference to "Junia" is female because that word seldom if ever appears as a shortened male name, and a native speaker of Greek like the fourth-century leader John Chrysostom in his homily on Romans treating 16:7 says, "What a fine women she must have been to be of note among the apostles." Is Junia of note among the apostles and Chrysostom but not among the curia?

Within evangelical circles I have heard even women insist that Priscilla did not teach Apollos as Acts 18:26 says. The plural verb,

---

8. John Paul II, *Mulieris dignitatem: On the Dignity and Vocation of Women, Apostolic Letter, August 15, 1988* (Washington, D.C.: Office of Publishing and Promotional Services, United States Catholic Conference, 1988).

9. Ibid., 102.

which includes both Aquila and Priscilla, is interpreted as a singular one referring only to the man Aquila because women are not to teach as Paul says in 1 Corinthians 14:34-35. The woman at the well does not proclaim the good news to her neighbors in Samaria as John 4:4-44 suggests; she only gives a testimony of what happened to her and thus cannot be seen as a "preacher" even though people believed in Christ on the basis of her testimony. Women are to be silent in the church as Paul says in 1 Corinthians. No woman should preside at the Lord's table, should prayerfully consecrate the bread and wine, because no verse in Scripture says a women presided at the supper. Yet the truth is that we do not know who presided at the table; that is not given to us by command or precedent in the New Testament.

Many women are excluded from taking positions of importance and power within the congregations, primarily on the basis of mistranslated and misunderstood biblical passages or silences. In some places known to me odd practices arise in regard to women's participation within such leadership roles. Sometimes they cannot pray, but can sing solos; sometimes they can lead singing but cannot announce the hymns. Many times they are allowed to teach only children, and never, ever to preach. The results of these kinds of arch-conservative positions are at times ludicrous because they are hilarious; at other times they bring so much pain that you hardly know how to respond. I offer only two examples, although many more could be supplied. Once when I spoke to a group of college-age Christians about the topic of women in the Church, I found that they were all agreed that women should keep silent, that women should not teach adults or preach to the assembled congregation. During lunch, the entire conversation was carried on by the young men. But about eight of those fellows had young women at their sides, who whispered in those men's ears the questions which they wanted asked. I will never lose that picture because it was so utterly sad. Here were bright college women speaking their minds to their men friends, but not participating in direct public discussion of the issues with the guest on campus. They were learning that they could silently determine the agenda for such discussions without having their own emotions, their own expressions, open for public commendation or rebuttle. It also amazed me that those young men could view themselves as authority figures when they were actually ventriloquists' dummies.

In another incident while I was in seminary, a friend of mine who was also a pastor talked to me about a practice which occurred at the meetings of his church board. A number of conservative Protestant churches have a group of local people, who with the pastor, determine some of the policies and actions of the congregation. Those boards are often totally male. My friend said that after two years of serving this church he had never known any important question to be settled at one board meeting. It was always tabled and then discussed with action at the next meeting. He praised that mature wisdom, the prayer and care these men used in their deliberations. But within a couple of weeks he came up to me somewhat sheepishly and told me a different story. At that time some parts of rural Oklahoma still had multi-party telephones rather than private ones. Sometimes eight or nine families would be on the same telephone line. One Monday morning after a Sunday evening board meeting, he picked up his phone and heard two wives of board members discussing the "important" issue and deciding how their husbands should vote at the next meeting. Instead of wisdom gained from the participation of all its members, his congregation had a shadow cabinet of women who influenced, perhaps even decided, most significant issues without ever speaking out in the actual debates or having to defend their arguments in a public forum.

Part of me sees the humor of these situations. Another part of me finds it terribly sad. Because many conservative Christian groups exclude women from places of decision making, many women of good sense, education, and good will either leave the churches they know, avoid most activities or learn to manipulate others from behind the scenes. There is even a dangerous kind of popular conservative Protestant literature in which women are told to use their sexual allures in marriage so that they can get whatever they want. Christian authors from Christian publishing houses teach a kind of perverse "submission" to husbands which is actually total dominance. Send the children to mother's; meet him in a negligee; make his sexual fantasies live and you can get the refrigerator he says is too expensive. The point is clear. You can follow Paul's advice and be a submissive wife and let your husband be the head of the house. Any man can be the head of the house, because you, the wife, can be the neck. Necks always turn heads.

For the life of me I cannot see how such uses of power serve the Church, Christ's body, which is sustained by his submissive death. If women are strong leaders, if they are gifted or well-educated for the positions needed, why not give them the jobs? Some of the best examples of clarity on these issues come from Fundamentalists or Evangelicals who are part of Pentecostal or Holiness traditions. Their emphasis upon the Spirit and gifts for ministry has led them to see clearly that if people have the needed the talents, they should be encouraged to do the work. For decades these communities have honored women in ministry and in many instances have found it bizarre not to employ such wonderful leaders for the kingdom. If all of us together can learn to read Scripture carefully, to investigate yet again the history of remarkable participation by women in various ministries of the Church, perhaps we can move back toward the truth of our shared heritage.[10]

I say this not because of twentieth-century feminism, which I respect but also find wanting. Such feminism at times urges women to take over some of the worst characteristics of obnoxious men as if that would provide a solution. I have known strong women who could well teach strong men how to lead, how to be compassionate, how to be submissive. But quiet, apparently compassionate treatment of the so-called fairer and weaker sex as if they are always fairer and weaker than men strikes me as condescending, lacking in Christian insight and Christian love.

It is not only gender difficulties which the Church faces in bringing all its parts into the process of upbuilding the whole. We also need to look within our ranks for those of different race, or different education, or different capacities so that the ministry of the whole Church can be brought to its fullest. Perhaps one of the most dangerous similarities which evangelical Protestants and Roman Catholics share is our Western concern for authority and credentialing. We try to draw the proper lines of authority so that improper people will not make inadequate decisions. Thus, too

---

10. Donald Dayton, *Theological Roots of Pentecostalism* (Grand Rapids, Mich.: Francis Asbury Press, 1987).

often we become social organizations which are paralyzed, incapable of responding to needs. We—especially those such as I who teach in seminaries where leaders are educated—make shopping lists of character traits, knowledge, and skills which will create the proper leader. I have no doubt that some processes like these are helpful and indeed necessary. But I am never sure that the ministry of the Church is enhanced to its fullest capacity when it requires ordained clergy, not female, not black, not uneducated, not too bombastic, not too crude, to take the place of Junia, Phoebe, and a bunch of bumbling fishermen like the apostles.

Again an example. The story is told of an Evangelical minister in a southern state who was preparing for the spring revival. He collected from the congregation, and from older records in the church files, a list of prospects, people who might be ready to become Christians. Then he announced that all those church members interested in making calls on the prospects should meet on Wednesday evening after prayer meeting. To his utter horror, a young man who was mentally retarded came to the meeting. Joe couldn't read, but he could memorize a few things if they were simple. He couldn't be taught any approach to a non-Christian as the rest of the class would be, for he wouldn't be able to follow it. What was to be done?

The preacher decided—in his wisdom—that he would give this young retarded man the toughest nuts to crack in this small, county seat town. If he gave Joe five names, Joe could memorize those because he knew nearly everyone in town. The first name was that of the county prosecutor, a man who had come from a Christian family, but after college had shown unmasked hostility toward the Church. His office was in the courthouse on the center square. The young retarded fellow had never been in that office; he had only seen the attorney at the repair shop where he worked or in the general store. So when he saw the secretary sitting there outside the main office and did not see the lawyer, he asked her where the fellow was. She said behind the door to her right, so he just walked in. He didn't know why that pretty lady was waiting out there, but he didn't want to wait. She hurriedly called the prosecutor on the intercom, apologized for not stopping this odd looking fellow, and the attorney said it was all right.

Joe got right to the point. "Do you want to be a Christian?"

he asked. The lawyer hemmed and hawed a bit, but let the young man know that he had no interest in being a Christian. "All right," the retarded man said, looking him straight in the eye, "Go to hell then. Just go to hell."

That kind of approach was never taught in any evangelism classes I have attended or taught. Nobody could be that dumb; nobody could be that insensitive. A young retarded man could. And now a prosecuting attorney is a Christian because he just couldn't get that fellow's words out of his mind. I have no doubt that his earlier training in Church played a large part in his return to the Church; other factors probably also were involved. But a young retarded man with no skills and no education, with all the wrong sensitivities lit the fire and moved the lawyer. And now a lawyer with his gifts can find his own place in ministry.

Both Protestants and Catholics need to widen their sense of ministry to include all the Church so that the work of Christ can be carried on by all parts of the body. The priesthood of all believers, a biblical concept found useful in Christian traditions of all stripes, needs to be emphasized again. The apostolic aspect of the Church in its ministry may well be seen in such wide parameters rather than in some small sense of succession. The work of ministry has its succession; people die and their places must be taken. Ordination must be given its due. There are reasons to set apart people for special tasks. But we must encourage ministry from all to all so that, as Paul says, indeed some may be won. John Paul II has recently insisted on the importance of evangelism, an emphasis that will be welcomed by conservative Protestants as a good sign. But if it is to be taken with seriousness, more ministry will need to be recognized than that limited to single, male, ordained priests.

Perhaps what we need is a deeper study of ordination and apostolic succession so that the needs of ministry become the primary focus, not the lines of authority and the concepts of office. I am neither opposed to ordination nor to considerations of authority, but they will not be the way to unleash ministry in its broadest and deepest manifestations within the Church and within the world. No one in their right mind would ordain a retarded man like Joe to ministry and give him a place of authority. Yet no ordained clergyman with the proper authority was able to minister to the lawyer the way Joe did. It is the priesthood of all that empowers the evangelization of all.

The early ecumenical efforts of this century moved in circles called Faith and Order, Life and Work. Eventually they overlapped and joined together to form the World Council of Churches. Now the participation of both Eastern Orthodox and Roman Catholic people has greatly broadened its scope, yet it has not left the little traditions behind. During these early years, a brilliant theologian from my own fellowship, William Robinson of the Churches of Christ in Great Britain, made remarkable contributions. He found important parts of his ministry defined by ecumenical involvements.

Whatever you think of National Council and World Council efforts—now too liberal, now too conservative—they have pointed out and continue to point out that one of the areas in which various traditions can come together is in projects which need our total assistance: world hunger, nuclear concerns, birth and abortion, AIDS, etc. There are ways in which ethicists from Roman Catholic and Protestant circles have been able to see similarities. Some years ago, obviously after Vatican II, James Gustafson insisted that there were signs of mutual understanding among Protestants and Catholics when it came to describing and living the Christian life. Yet he noted both that great gulfs have divided Catholic and Protestants on ethics and that few Catholics have paid much attention to the ethics of Protestant Evangelicals or Fundamentalists.[11]

The study of ethics among conservative Protestants is not marked by one particular approach. I have my own strong opinions in these areas. Although I applaud Roman Catholics and Protestant Evangelicals who worship and work together, I am concerned about one similarity between Roman Catholic and conservative Protestant ethics. Any honest interpreter of the mass of literature must note that there is a mutual interest in natural law between the two groups, indeed a type of ethics which works vigorously from a doctrine of creation toward what specific ac-

---

11. James Gustafson, *Protestant and Roman Catholic Ethics* (Chicago: The University of Chicago Press, 1975). His first chapter was part of the Tuohy lectures at John Carroll in 1975.

tivities Christians should choose. What bothers some interpreters of Fundamentalist or Evangelical ethics is a kind of biblical legalism which creates long lists of things to be done and to be avoided. That is not the issue to which I refer here. Earlier I noted that Roman Catholics have a stronger doctrine of creation than many conservative Protestants, one which can be of great help in strengthening conservative Protestants and moving them away from incessant concern with creationism and evolution. That God is Creator and that the world is God's creation we would all confess. But here I raise a caution that we all need to remember. This is broken, fallen creation which we now see. In its present state it is capable of giving only hints of the glory of God. Making creation or natural law the basis of apologetics or ethics entails a basic flaw. Creation and natural law tell us far less about God than God told us in the incarnation of Jesus of Nazareth. That truth is one of the major thrusts of both Scripture and Tradition, one which both C. S. Lewis and Thomas Aquinas knew.

The tendency has existed within Roman Catholic and Protestant Evangelical ethics to read a good many guides for Christian conduct off the natural world, indeed from what is called natural law. An evangelical figure like C. S. Lewis could make that point an important one in his apologetic for Christianity. In those early views he found foundational principles in every culture and religion which had to go back to the divine creator.[12] Timothy O'Connell, in the recent revision of his clear introduction to Roman Catholic ethics, takes most of the book to point out how important natural law is to the enterprise. Although that approach has been under attack within various Roman Catholic circles, he still sees it as the basis for knowing the good and doing it.[13] And it certainly has the weight of Thomas Aquinas behind it.

There are at least two major criticisms of such an approach, however, which come from both Protestant and Catholic circles. First, the biblical basis of a natural law ethic is tiny. A defender of that view might find Paul in Romans 1–2 and Galatians 5 supporting it. The apostle does argue that the sense of God's invi-

12. C. S. Lewis, in his *The Abolition of Man* (New York: Macmillan, 1947), provides an appendix of natural laws that he senses are shared by many cultures.

13. Timothy O'Connell, *Principles for a Catholic Morality,* rev. ed. (San Francisco: Harper & Row, 1990).

sible nature, his eternal power and deity, is clearly present in nature, so clear in fact that the Gentiles have a law within them so that their conscience or their "conflicting thoughts accuse or perhaps excuse them" on judgment day. He also finds that the "fruits of the Spirit" have no law against them. Yet the difficulty is a plain and honest one. Natural law is not spelled out in any detail in these passages so that it can be a guide to ethics.

The second criticism follows similar lines but is itself much stronger. Even if one were undeterred by the lack of biblical basis, the problem of spelling out the details of natural law still exists. It is so frozen in the cultural patterns of any given time that it varies dramatically from age to age. It does not seem possible to make it clear enough to be the foundation of any telling ethic. There has been interminable argument about the content of natural law and an inability to make it a tool which can be used in public debate where theological premises are out of court.[14]

In my judgment the most promising approach to ethics is the work of Alasdair MacIntyre and Stanley Hauerwas. The first a Roman Catholic and the second a conserving Methodist, they have insisted that within a context in which foundationalism is dead, in which an appeal to an obvious open public forum where everyone has the same assumptions and basic principles is impossible, it is best to accept the confessions of the Christian community as the basis of personhood, character and ethical activity. Because even the sciences are now aware that there is no neutral foundation from which any and all can argue basic beliefs and moral acts, it is necessary to learn the narratives of the Christian community from inside its worship and life. From that web of belief we can then work on who we are and what we should do. Hauerwas has been charged with sectarianism and thus often sounds too conservative for some, including his former teacher,[15] yet both

14. Russell Hittinger, *A Critique of the New Natural Law Theory* (Notre Dame, Ind.: Notre Dame University Press, 1987). Hittinger does not attack O'Connell, but he does decimate the works of Germain Grisez and John Finnis, two Roman Catholic natural law ethicists.

15. Stanley Hauerwas, "Introduction," *Christian Existence Today: Essays on Church, World and Living in Between* (Durham, N.C.: The Labyrinth Press, 1988) responds to James Gustafson's charges, "The Sectarian Temptation: Reflections on Theology, the Church and the University," *Proceedings of the Catholic Theological Society,* 40 (1985) 83–94 that he is a sectarian, by saying, "I do not blame

these authors offer a well-articulated concept of Christian identity and suggest kinds of conduct which are appropriate to Christian claims. Their concern for the development of character within community encourages hope for Christian involvement in various ethical problems and also stands against the inability of many ethicists to find ways to stop their incessant questioning and get on with it. MacIntyre's and Hauerwas' views are criticized by those who continue to search for a neutral public square in which every commitment, every belief, will somehow be judged by a neutral, informed set of values. That chimera will help none of us.

We are much more likely to find ways in which we can work together for the betterment of the human condition if we learn to worship together and to define Christian character and deeds from the life of Jesus and the early Christian communities as well as catholic Christian Tradition. Living a Christ-like life, attempting to treat people as he did, will always be a shared goal. The plight of the hungry and homeless, the drug-infested, the tragically pregnant, the sick and dying cannot be ignored if we are followers of Christ. The celibacy of Catholic priests may lead to the disheartening failures of certain endeavors where a wayward sexual desire or love of money destroys faith and effort. But the answer is not to have all priests marry. There are places in this world where no married person with sense will go because spouse and children would be engangered. When so many conservative Protestants have only married ministers, there is need to be supportive both of the single people in those traditions who want to minister and of the Catholics who are already there ministering. We cannot waste the resources of the Church by keeping ourselves separate from these goals in interminable arguments about ministry. We need to work together.

There are already areas in which Roman Catholics and Protestant Evangelicals have worked alongside each other. Although I did not find the furor over *The Last Temptation of Christ* al-

anyone for approaching my work (or [John Howard] Yoder's) with a good deal of caution and skepticism. What I find unfair, however, is the assumption that my critic has a hold on my task by calling me a 'sectarian.' Show me where I am wrong about God, Jesus, the limits of liberalism, the nature of the virtues, or the doctrine of the church—but do not shortcut that task by calling me a sectarian'' (8).

ways well-targeted or sure of its war, I did find the television clips and interviews interesting because it was so clear that both Roman Catholics and conservative Protestants were involved together. What was seen as an attack on Jesus Christ was an attack which wounded all his followers. I am convinced that within many settings, particularly urban ones, there is a myriad of problems which can become a part of a mutual agenda.

Even in places like the South, unexpected by self-appointed leaders of culture, there are interesting prospects. In my home town of Johnson City, Tennessee, the campus ministries of East Tennessee State University, including conservative Protestant and Roman Catholic efforts, have found a number of ways in which they have been able to work together. Critical ethical issues like nuclear war or world hunger have brought students to lectures, services, even small marches in which they have made their mutual concerns known. To my happy amazement in recent months the Roman Catholic parish and one of the Methodist churches even found ways to have joint workshops on congregational vitality. I can remember when there were "apparent" problems in the late 1970s with children's soccer teams because some of the kids were "Christian" and some were "Catholic." A few of the parents from conservative Protestant congregations felt strange around the "Catholics." Yet in some important ways these local Southern people, dominated by Scotch-Irish heritage with its conservative Protestant roots, have moved far beyond what is necessarily envisioned or encouraged by their leaders. If we can learn to worship and to work with each other in the best of Christ's spirit, some of our varied views of devotion, ethics, ministry, etc., can be cherished as reflections of God's untold riches. Not all, but enough that our divisions may cease to be a hindrance to the kingdom of God.

# Conclusion

In the opinion of many observers conservative Protestants and Roman Catholics have little in common. They do not worship together and too seldom find projects for the common good in which they can participate together. Their histories have divided them for so long that much seems hopeless. It is not only in Northern Ireland that the two groups have grappled to the death. Where violence does not mark weekly existence, there can still be misunderstanding and a sense of unease. Each group has asked about the other: are people like that really Christian?

No person who looks at the realities will think that these two traditions, so often divided within their own ranks and suspicious of others, will soon embrace as sisters and brothers. But there are ways in which some of the gains of recent years, particularly in the United States, can be made significant achievements. One avenue is to make a maxim of minimalist views. When I gave these lectures at Cleveland in 1988 it was so easy to think in terms of the rivalry between the Cleveland Browns and the Denver Broncos and forget that the game was football, the teams were football teams, and the players were football players. Those descriptions are not unrealistic, nor are they so minimalist that there are no characteristics which can be called to our attention. In fact if you forget that the game is football, you miss the point.

None of us doubt that there will always be a type of one-true-Church mentality which marks conservative Protestants and Roman Catholics. But as Augustine noted such people are often apparently ''big'' frogs croaking in realistically ''small'' ponds.

There are those of reputable standing in each group who recognize that Christ's Church has boundaries they do not know, that its members are comprised of those whom God has added, not merely those who are most like our own particular congregation and its faithful friends. Vatican II opened the way for Catholics to recognize other groups and individuals as Christians, ones who are not officially recognizable as living within the boundary of Roman Catholicism. And some conservative Protestants see clearly that their band does not exhaust the Church.

If we use the Nicene-Constantinopolitan Creed as a standard of reference, the most ecumenical of all the creeds of Christendom, one in line with biblical insights contextualized for the fourth century, we find fewer differences between Protestant Evangelicals and Roman Catholics than we would expect. That creed does not teach us to concentrate on ordained ministry in apostolic succession. It does not set up restricted worship. It gives us the content of the faith in a skeletal structure which is acceptable in both Protestant Evangelical and Roman Catholic circles. Both see Christian faith as the worship and glorification of the Father, the Son, and the Holy Spirit. Each confesses one, holy, catholic and apostolic Church, Eucharist, baptism, resurrection, and the life to come. When there are so many religions and value systems on this earth which are obviously not Christian, why is it that we Evangelical Protestants and Roman Catholics so often insist on thinking of ourselves only as different, even separate groups?

The answers to that are rather straightforward. We grow up within different orders of ministry and different liturgies, we sometimes attend different schools or colleges and live in different neighborhoods. We often remain separate. But when we are brought together for whatever purposes, we often find that we share many things in common. You may have neighbors or friends who are conservative Protestants, people you met near home or at work. And you have found that they don't have horns and tails, although they do have what you consider decidedly bizarre views on some things. Those Roman Catholics who had watched my father minister in a small West Virginia community did not agree with him at every point. But over time they could not see anything untoward in asking him if he would consider becoming their priest. That request was decidedly odd to a number of faithful

Catholics, but it was not odd to those asking the question. While I was a doctoral student at Yale University, one of my colleagues concentrating on the early Church was an Irish Catholic priest from Boston, Joe Gibbon: mouth, cigar, booze, and all. Knowing primarily conservative Protestants from the Midwest, I had never known anyone like him before. But after a few months I could find little about him which was essentially odd. He believed and practiced the faith and was committed to the Lord and his Church. That made him much more like me than were many of my mainline Protestant friends, even though a number of my Fundamentalist and Evangelical friends might find his sense of things utterly bizarre. The point is a simple one, but all the more provocative for its simplicity. When conservative Protestants and Roman Catholics come to know each other in groups which concentrate on our central characteristics, we find out that as Christians we share a great deal with each other.

That is a grand beginning which must be given its due. No sniffing from upturned noses. No sidewise glances or smirks. Little it may be, but great are its implications. To confess that the body of Christ is greater than the earthly allegiances we know even within our Church groups at the same time that we profess our congregations to be true Churches is often a new insight for theologians and clerics. Yet those who have lived in neighborhoods with good Christian people of other traditions have recognized these truths for decades if not centuries.

We must, however, find ways to expand that grand beginning. We could easily spend our time emphasizing the differences which separate us; or we can emphasize the features which make us whole. We do rely on the Bible within Tradition, an interdependence which still allows the Bible to foster reform. Since Vatican II Roman Catholics have found ways to question traditions which see themselves as authorities equal to Scripture and not judged by it, while conservative Protestans are rediscovering the inescapable context of Tradition and traditions within which they have received and interpret Scripture. Each group has doctrines which complement each other best when the two groups are viewed together. Even within questions of ecclesiology and authority, the deepest sense of fullness in Christian faith is found in considerations of each others' positions, whether that be the doctrine of

Scripture and Tradition, or questions of ministry and sacrament.

We must not ignore the differences for they can be important. If Mary rises almost to the place of a fourth member in the Trinity, Protestant Evangelicals will insist that something is amiss. When individual interpretation of Scripture functions as the only norm within the Church, Roman Catholics will warn that something is awry. What we must continue to do is emphasize our basic oneness, our sense of divinity and purpose as found in the gospel. No great breakthroughs should be expected, but at various places in important first steps simple Christianity can arise. It will not be easy; it will demand sacrifice from each. But the goal of the oneness of Christ's Church, the recognition of catholic Christian Faith is significant enough to pursue the risks.

Roman Catholics and conservative Protestants are Christians; we share in each others' lives because we are sisters and brothers in Christ. Nothing can change that because it is God's reality, not ours. We do not construct our unity; it is a gift from God. We must unwrap it, take possession of it. We sometimes make nearly every aspect of our diversity prominent, but those are not the ultimate features of Christian community. In God's providence, even the visible churches are united, set apart for Christ's use, indwelt by the Spirit, universal in their scope, and dedicated to the irrepeatable conditions of their origins passed on within faithful Tradition. My only hope is that we come to recognize that those aspects are more important than any superficial differences that seem so obvious. At the end, they will pale before the one, holy, catholic and apostolic Church, of which we are all a part. Indeed, let our prayers and actions express the spirit of the 1970 decree on ecumenism: "our gratitude for the partial unity already obtained, our regret for the divisions which still remain and our firm resolve to do everything possible to overcome them, and finally our humble petition to the Lord to hasten the day when we will be able to celebrate together the mystery of the Body and Blood of Christ."[1]

---

1. *Vatican Council II: Conciliar and Post Conciliar Documents,* ed. Austin Flannery, O.P., New Rev. Ed. (Northport, N.Y.: Costello Publishing Company, 1984) 39. *Dans ces derniers temps,* 10, 507.

# Scripture Index

# Subject and Name Index